Thomas Hennell

Hydraulic and other Tables

For Purposes cf Sewage and Water-Supply

Thomas Hennell

Hydraulic and other Tables
For Purposes of Sewage and Water-Supply

ISBN/EAN: 9783337141455

Printed in Europe, USA, Canada, Australia, Japan

Cover: Foto ©ninafisch / pixelio.de

More available books at **www.hansebooks.com**

HYDRAULIC AND OTHER TABLES,

FOR PURPOSES OF

SEWERAGE AND WATER-SUPPLY.

BY

THOMAS HENNELL,

M. INST. C.E.

LONDON:

E. & F. N. SPON, 16, CHARING CROSS.

NEW YORK: 35, MURRAY STREET.

1884.

PREFACE.

It has been found that the Engineering Pocket Books in most general use give comparatively little information

Every precaution has been taken, as far as possible, to guard against errors both in the calculations and printing. If however, notwithstanding, any mistakes should be discovered, the author will be greatly obliged by having them pointed out to him.

6, DELAHAY STREET, WESTMINSTER,
November 1883.

PREFACE.

———◦◇◦———

IT has been found that the Engineering Pocket Books in most general use give comparatively little information relating to Sewerage and Water Supply. And even the large and valuable works of the late Mr. Beardmore and others contain somewhat abridged Tables applicable to the calculations most frequently required in designing and carrying out works of moderate size.

The Tables in this book have been calculated from time to time by the author to meet his own requirements. Thinking it probable that other engineers will have experienced the same want as himself, he has now been induced to make them public. The greater part have been used in manuscript for some years; but a few additional Tables have been recently added in order to make the work more complete.

Every precaution has been taken, as far as possible, to guard against errors both in the calculations and printing. If however, notwithstanding, any mistakes should be discovered, the author will be greatly obliged by having them pointed out to him.

6, DELAHAY STREET, WESTMINSTER,
November 1883.

CONTENTS.

——◆◦◆——

DESCRIPTION AND REMARKS ON THE USE OF THE TABLES.

TABLES I. and II. show the quantities of water in gallons per foot contained in pipes, wells, tanks, &c., of given dimensions, and require no explanation.

Tables III. and IV. give the discharge in gallons per minute of water passing through sluices and over weirs under ordinary conditions. Correction is required in case of bell-mouthed or specially formed orifices, and also where there is any considerable velocity of current in approaching the outlets, but the notes at the head of the Tables, to which attention should be directed, will enable this to be made with sufficient accuracy for most practical purposes.

Table V. shows the velocity and discharge under varying conditions of flow in circular sewers and conduits, from 9 inches to 6 feet in diameter.

In designing and carrying out sewerage works, it is important to know not only the maximum carrying capacity of the sewers, but also the effect produced by the much smaller quantity which will be generally flowing through them. This is essential in order to ascertain whether flushing will be required, and if so, what quantity of water will be needed for the purpose. The Table consequently shows, not only the maximum discharge and velocity of each kind of sewer under the most favourable circumstances, but also the discharge and velocity of the same sewers when full to one-half, one quarter, and one-eighth only of their heights respectively. If a sewer

should at any time run quite full, its discharge will be
somewhat less than that indicated in the fourth column,
the velocity of current being in that case considerably
diminished by friction against the top.   With any circular conduit the velocity when full is exactly the same,
and the discharge just double that when half-full ; the pre-
cise figures for a sewer running full may therefore be
ascertained, if required, from the third column of Table
by doubling the discharge.

A velocity of 150 feet per minute, or $2\frac{1}{2}$ feet per
second, is generally considered sufficient to remove all
obstacles of the ordinary character found in sewers.   The
quantity of water required to produce this velocity in
each case is given in the last column of the same Table,
and will be found especially useful in designing flushing
arrangements.

Table VI. gives precisely similar information for egg-
shaped sewers, as Table V. for circular sewers.

Table VII. gives the discharge of pipes from $\frac{3}{4}$-inch
to 3 feet diameter, when running full at various inclinations or pressures.   It should be remembered that the
velocity of water passing through a line of pipes of any
considerable length depends not on the inclination of any
particular section, but on the hydraulic gradient through-
out, or ratio of head of water to length of pipe; the
"head" being the difference of level between the surface
at or above the upper end of the pipe, and that of the
cistern or pond into which it delivers, or if it has a free
outlet, the lower end of the pipe itself.   This velocity,
except for slightly increased friction at bends, is entirely
independent of the course of the pipes, whether laid at a
uniform inclination or otherwise, also whether commencing
at or below the upper surface and discharging, if not
freely, at or below the lower surface.

The formula which has been used in the calculations

for Tables V., VI., VII., is that known as Eytelwein's Formula, which is the basis of the tables contained in Beardmore's 'Manual of Hydrology.' The formula used in Neville's Tables, and those found in Hurst's and Molesworth's Pocket Books, gives generally rather higher results: varying in fact from about 20 per cent. higher in the case of the sharpest inclinations quoted in Tables V. and VI. herein to 5 per cent. in case of the flattest in the same Tables. And referring to Table VII., Neville's formula would give results varying from about 25 per cent. higher at the top, to from 2 to 5 per cent. lower at the foot of each page.

Except with very flat inclinations, it may therefore be fairly assumed that the results here given are somewhat within the mark, and this is especially the case with the larger sewers and pipes.

Table VIII. is intended to assist in designing the capacity of sewers, and shows at a glance the quantity of sewage, irrespective of rain and surface water, which should be allowed for given populations. In certain cases (see note at foot of Table), the allowance for rain may also be calculated on the basis of population with the help of the last column of the Table, but under ordinary circumstances this should be taken in proportion to area as shown by Table IX., next following.

Table IX. shows the quantity of water due to rainfall over given areas, and the quantities in gallons per minute, when running off at different rates of flow. The latter columns of the Table are intended for calculating the capacity of sewers ; and the second and third columns for estimating the quantity of water that can be collected from areas and gathering grounds for irrigation or water supply. The areas dealt with range from 100 square feet (representing the roof of a small building) to one square mile.

Tables X., XI., XII., are rainfall Tables, extracted principally from those prepared by Mr. Symons, for the Annual Reports of the Meteorological Society. That showing the monthly distribution at Edinburgh is, however, taken from figures contained in a valuable paper on the water supply of that city, by Mr. A. Leslie, C.E., which was read at the Institution of Civil Engineers last session.

Tables XIII. and XIV. are intended to facilitate the preparation of preliminary reports and rough estimates for works of water supply, and show the approximate dimensions of reservoirs, filter beds, main pipes, pumping machinery, &c., required for the supply of given populations. It is not of course asserted that the constant numbers assumed in the headings of the columns are universally applicable; and some few, e. g. 100 feet lift to be pumped, are necessarily arbitrary. But the differences due to variations in these conditions can be ascertained generally either by inspection or by a short calculation, and results may be thus arrived at with much greater facility than if the Tables were not available.

Table XV. gives results of analyses of potable waters. To engineers and others, not constantly or very frequently engaged in investigating the quality of water, the figures presented by an analysis convey little information without some readily available standard of comparison. This it is endeavoured to afford by means of this Table, which contains the results of analyses of well-known waters from nearly every description of source.

It is not proposed here to give any opinion on the much disputed question of the determination of organic matter in water. This was formerly attempted to be shown by the "loss on ignition" of the dissolved solid matters, and subsequently by the "oxygen required to oxidise oxidisable matter" therein. Both these methods have

been generally abandoned, but other two are still in use.
The first of these, known as the combustion process, and
adopted by Dr. Frankland and others, is to ascertain the
quantities of carbon, nitrogen, and ammonia set free
from the solid matter during combustion, and which are
believed to be organic carbon and nitrogen. Dr. Frankland
in his reports also gives always the nitrogen found in the
solid residue as nitrates, which are mineral not organic
substances, but are liable to have derived their origin from
organic substance since disappeared.

The second method of determining the organic matter
is called the " ammonia process," and consists in a distilla-
tion of the water by means of which the nitrogen contained
in any organic substances is necessarily turned into ammonia ; and this is called " free " or " albumenoid " ammonia according as it is evolved in the first or second
stage of the process.

As both these methods are still in use by eminent
chemists, it is thought desirable to give results of each of
them. The first nine columns of the Table accordingly contain (1) the total solid matter dissolved in the water ;
next the portion of this total which consists of earthy salts,
commonly known' as " hardness," and divided into (2)
" temporary " hardness, i. e. removable by boiling the
water ; and (3) " permanent ; " (4) the total hardness ; (5)
the chlorine ; (6) organic carbon ; (7) organic nitrogen ;
(8) ammonia ; and (9) the nitrogen contained in nitrates :
all these being obtained by the combustion process. The
whole of this part of the Table is from analyses made
principally by Dr. Frankland, and which have been
published from time to time in the Reports of the Rivers
Pollution Commissioners and other official documents. In
columns 10 and 11 will be found the quantities of free
and albumenoid ammonia evolved by the ammonia process, from specimens of the same waters ; and for the

information contained in these columns the author is
indebted to Professor Wanklyn, the inventor of that
process.

Tables XVI. and XVII. give the quantities of brickwork
per yard in sewers, culverts, &c., and require no explanation.

Table XVIII. gives the weight per yard of cast-iron
pipes adapted to different pressures of water. These
weights have been arrived at not by theoretical calculation,
but by a careful comparison of the specifications and recent
practice of experienced engineers. They agree, however,
nearly with the calculated strengths as given by Mr. Box
in his Hydraulic Tables. The weights for various safe
heads found in Table 14 of Beardmore's ' Manual of Hydrology,' are certainly insufficient according to recent
practice.

Table XIX. gives the weights per yard of lead service
pipes of five different qualities as described in the note
appended to the Table.

TABLE I.—QUANTITY of WATER contained in PIPES, WELLS, and CIRCULAR TANKS, per foot in length or depth.

Diam.	Contents.	Diam.		Contents.	Diam.	Contents.	Diam.	Contents.
inches.	gals. per foot	ft.	in.	gals. per foot	feet.	gals. per foot	feet.	gals. per foot
¼	·005	1	9	15·0	11	594	90	39,758
½	·008	2	0	19·6	12	707	100	49,088
¾	·019	2	3	24·8	13	829	110	59,396
1	·034	2	6	30·7	14	962	120	70,685
1½	·076	2	9	37·1	15	1,104	130	82,956
2	·135	3	0	44·2	16	1,256	140	96,211
2½	·212	3	3	51·8	17	1,418	150	110,447
3	·305	3	6	60·2	18	1,590	160	125,664
4	·54	3	9	69·0	19	1,772	170	141,862
5	·85	4	0	78·5	20	1,963	180	159,044
6	1·22	4	6	99·4	25	3,068	190	177,206
7	1·66	5	0	122·7	30	4,418	200	196,350
8	2·17	5	6	148·5	35	6,013	250	306,796
9	2·75	6	0	176·7	40	7,854	300	441,788
10	3·39	6	6	207·4	45	9,940	350	601,322
11	4·12	7	0	240·5	50	12,272	400	785,400
12	4·91	7	6	276·1	55	14,850	500	1,227,190
13	5·75	8	0	314·2	60	17,671	600	1,767,150
14	6·67	8	6	354·7	65	20,740	700	2,405,290
15	7·67	9	0	397·6	70	24,053	800	3,141,600
16	8·72	9	6	443·0	75	27,611	900	3,975,750
18	11·04	10	0	490·9	80	31,416	1000	4,908,750

TABLE II.—QUANTITY of WATER contained in SQUARE CISTERNS or TANKS, per foot in depth.

Length of Side.		Contents.	Length of Side.		Contents.	Length of Side.	Contents.	Length of Side.	Contents.
ft.	in.	gals. per foot	ft.	in.	gals. per foot	feet	gals. per foot	feet	gals. per foot
1	0	6·25	6	0	205	25	3,906	90	50,625
1	6	14·06	7	0	306	30	5,625	100	62,500
2	0	25·00	8	0	400	35	7,756	125	156,250
2	6	39·06	9	0	506	40	10,000	150	140,625
3	0	56·25	10	0	625	45	12,656	200	250,000
3	6	77·56	11	0	756	50	15,625	300	562,500
4	0	100·00	12	0	900	60	20,500	400	1,000,000
4	6	126·56	15	0	1,406	70	30,625	500	1,562,500
5	0	156·25	20	0	2,500	80	40,000	1000	6,250,000

TABLE III.—FLOW of WATER through SLUICES and OPENINGS.

NOTE.—The "Head of Water" in the Table must represent the depth from the surface to the centre of the opening; or if the opening be submerged, then the difference of level between the surfaces above and below.

If the opening be bell-mouthed, or be a sluice having curved side walls properly tapering inwards to the narrowest part, the discharge will be greater than that shown by the Table, to the extent of, in case of the best form of opening, about 50 per cent.

Head of Water.		Discharge per Square Foot in Area of Opening.	Head of Water.		Discharge per Square Foot in Area of Opening.	Head of Water.		Discharge per Square Foot in Area of Opening.	Head of Water.		Discharge per Square Foot in Area of Opening.
ft.	in.	galls. per minute	ft.	in.	galls. per minute	ft.	in.	galls. per minute	ft.	in.	gals. per minute
	½	382	2	3	2,813	8	3	5,385	16	6	7,616
	1	541	2	6	2,964	8	6	5,466	17	0	7,731
	1½	663	2	9	3,110	8	9	5,546	17	6	7,844
	2	765	3	0	3,248	9	0	5,625	18	0	7,956
	2½	856	3	3	3,379	9	3	5,702	18	6	8,064
	3	937	3	6	3,507	9	6	5,779	19	0	8,173
	3½	1,014	3	9	3,631	9	9	5,854	19	6	8,280
	4	1,082	4	0	3,751	10	0	5,929	20	0	8,385
	5	1,210	4	3	3,865	10	3	6,004	21	0	8,590
	6	1,326	4	6	3,977	10	6	6,075	22	0	8,796
	7	1,432	4	9	4,086	10	9	6,148	23	0	8,991
	8	1,530	5	0	4,192	11	0	6,219	24	0	9,184
	9	1,624	5	3	4,295	11	3	6,288	25	0	9,375
	10	1,712	5	6	4,398	11	6	6,358	26	0	9,558
	11	1,794	5	9	4,495	11	9	6,427	27	0	9,744
1	0	1,875	6	0	4,592	12	0	6,495	28	0	9,920
1	1	1,951	6	3	4,687	12	6	6,628	30	0	10,269
1	2	2,025	6	6	4,779	13	0	6,759	32	0	10,605
1	3	2,096	6	9	4,872	13	6	6,888	34	0	10,933
1	4	2,165	7	0	4,960	14	0	7,015	36	0	11,253
1	5	2,231	7	3	5,048	14	6	7,139	38	0	11,557
1	6	2,296	7	6	5,135	15	0	7,262	40	0	11,857
1	9	2,480	7	9	5,219	15	6	7,382	45	0	12,577
2	0	2,651	8	0	5,302	16	0	7,502	50	0	13,256

TABLE IV.—FLOW of WATER over WEIRS.

NOTE.—The "Depth" must represent difference in level between the sill of the weir and the surface of still water above it. If the water approaches the weir with a current having a perceptible velocity, the discharge will be greater than that shown by the Table to an extent depending on the velocity; a velocity of 2 feet per second will be equivalent generally to about half an inch, and a velocity of 3 feet per second to about three-quarters of an inch additional depth.

Depth.	Discharge per Inch in Width.	Depth.	Discharge per Inch in Width.	Depth.	Discharge per Inch in Width.	Depth.		Discharge per Inch in Width.
inches	gals. per min.	inches	gals. per min.	inches	gals. per min.	ft.	in.	gals. per min.
$\frac{1}{4}$	·334	$4\frac{1}{4}$	22·37	$10\frac{1}{4}$	87·5	2	1	334
$\frac{5}{16}$	·467	$4\frac{1}{4}$	23·39	$10\frac{1}{2}$	90·8	2	2	354
$\frac{3}{8}$	·613	$4\frac{3}{8}$	24·44	$10\frac{3}{4}$	94·1	2	3	374
$\frac{1}{2}$	·944	$4\frac{1}{2}$	25·49	11	97·4	2	4	395
$\frac{5}{8}$	1·329	$4\frac{5}{8}$	26·56	$11\frac{1}{4}$	100·7	2	5	417
$\frac{3}{4}$	1·734	$4\frac{3}{4}$	27·64	$11\frac{1}{2}$	104·1	2	6	439
$\frac{7}{8}$	2·185	$4\frac{7}{8}$	28·74	$11\frac{3}{4}$	107·5	2	7	461
1	2·670	5	29·85	12	111·0	2	8	483
$1\frac{1}{8}$	3·185	$5\frac{1}{8}$	30·97	$12\frac{1}{2}$	118·0	2	9	506
$1\frac{1}{4}$	3·818	$5\frac{1}{4}$	32·12	13	125·1	2	10	529
$1\frac{3}{8}$	4·305	$5\frac{3}{8}$	33·26	$13\frac{1}{2}$	132·5	2	11	553
$1\frac{1}{2}$	4·905	$5\frac{1}{2}$	34·44	14	139·8	3	0	577
$1\frac{5}{8}$	5·531	$5\frac{5}{8}$	35·62	$14\frac{1}{2}$	147·4	3	1	601
$1\frac{3}{4}$	6·167	$5\frac{3}{4}$	36·85	15	155·1	3	2	625
$1\frac{7}{8}$	6·855	$5\frac{7}{8}$	38·02	$15\frac{1}{2}$	163·0	3	3	650
2	7·552	6	39·24	16	170·9	3	4	675
$2\frac{1}{8}$	8·27	$6\frac{1}{8}$	41·72	$16\frac{1}{2}$	179·0	3	5	701
$2\frac{1}{4}$	9·01	$6\frac{1}{2}$	44·25	17	187·1	3	6	727
$2\frac{3}{8}$	9·77	$6\frac{3}{4}$	46·82	$17\frac{1}{2}$	195·5	3	7	753
$2\frac{1}{2}$	10·55	7	49·45	18	203·9	3	8	779
$2\frac{5}{8}$	11·36	$7\frac{1}{4}$	52·12	$18\frac{1}{2}$	212·3	3	9	806
$2\frac{3}{4}$	12·18	$7\frac{1}{2}$	54·84	19	221·1	3	10	833
$2\frac{7}{8}$	13·02	$7\frac{3}{4}$	57·61	$19\frac{1}{2}$	229·8	3	11	860
3	13·87	8	60·41	20	238·8	4	0	888
$3\frac{1}{8}$	14·75	$8\frac{1}{4}$	62·54	$20\frac{1}{2}$	247·6	4	1	915
$3\frac{1}{4}$	15·64	$8\frac{1}{2}$	66·17	21	256·9	4	2	944
$3\frac{3}{8}$	16·55	$8\frac{3}{4}$	69·11	$21\frac{1}{2}$	265·9	4	3	972
$3\frac{1}{2}$	17·48	9	72·09	22	275·5	4	4	1000
$3\frac{5}{8}$	18·42	$9\frac{1}{4}$	75·12	$22\frac{1}{2}$	284·8	4	6	1060
$3\frac{3}{4}$	19·39	$9\frac{1}{2}$	78·18	23	294·4	4	8	1120
$3\frac{7}{8}$	20·37	$9\frac{3}{4}$	81·29	$23\frac{1}{2}$	303·9	4	10	1180
4	21·36	10	84·43	24	313·9	5	0	1240

TABLE V.—VELOCITY and DISCHARGE per MINUTE in CIRCULAR SEWERS, with Water flowing at various depths.

Diameter 9 Inches.

Inclination.	One-eighth. (1⅛ Inch.)		One-quarter. (2¼ Inches.)		One-half. (4½ Inches.)		Seven-eighths. (Maximum Discharge.)		Quantity required to give Velocity of 150 Feet per Minute.
	Velocity.	Discharge.	Velocity.	Discharge.	Velocity.	Discharge.	Velocity.	Discharge.	
feet per mile	feet	gallons	feet	gallons	feet	gallons.	feet	gallons	gallons
1 in 20 — 264	300	58	420	225	550	755	600	1535	:
1 ,, 30 — 176	246	48	344	105	447	615	490	1245	:
1 ,, 40 — 132	212	40	296	158	387	530	424	1085	:
1 ,, 50 — 105·6	190	37	266	143	346	475	380	975	:
1 ,, 66 — 80	166	33	230	122	302	415	330	845	:
1 ,, 80 — 66	151	30	209	112	275	377	300	768	30
1 ,, 100 — 52·8	134	26	187	100	244	330	267	682	40
1 ,, 132 — 40	117	22	164	88	213	293	232	594	60
1 ,, 165 — 32	105	20	146	78	190	261	208	532	85
1 ,, 200 — 26·4	95	18	133	71	173	238	190	487	125
1 ,, 264 — 20	83	16	115	62	151	207	165	422	200
1 ,, 330 — 16	74	14	103	55	134	184	148	378	:
1 ,, 440 — 12	64	12	89	48	115	158	128	327	:
1 ,, 528 — 10	58	11	82	44	106	146	116	291	:

Depth of Flow in Proportion to Height of Sewer.

Velocity and Discharge per Minute in Circular Sewers, with Water flowing at various depths.

Diameter 12 Inches.

Inclination.	One-eighth. (1¼ Inch.)		One-quarter. (3 Inches.)		One-half. (6 Inches.)		Seven-eighths. (Maximum Discharge.)		Quantity required to give Velocity of 150 Feet per Minute.
	Velocity.	Discharge.	Velocity.	Discharge.	Velocity.	Discharge.	Velocity.	Discharge.	
feet per mile	feet	gallons	feet	gallons	feet	gallons	feet	gallons	gallons
1 in 30 — 176	284	98	396	380	520	1,275	565	2580	..
1 " 40 — 132	247	86	342	330	446	1,100	490	2235	..
1 " 50 — 105·6	220	76	303	292	400	980	438	2000	..
1 " 66 — 80	192	66	268	260	348	850	380	1730	..
1 " 80 — 66	173	60	243	235	316	725	346	1580	33
1 " 100 — 52·8	155	53	220	212	282	690	309	1410	45
1 " 132 — 40	135	46	188	181	246	600	270	1230	69
1 " 165 — 32	121	42	169	162	220	540	241	1100	96
1 " 200 — 26·4	110	38	151	145	200	490	219	1000	135
1 " 264 — 20	96	33	134	130	174	425	190	865	212
1 " 330 — 16	85	29	119	115	155	380	170	780	320
1 " 440 — 12	74	25	103	99	135	331	147	670	..
1 " 528 — 10	67	23	94	90	123	300	135	615	..
1 " 660 — 8	60	21	84	81	110	270	120	550	..

VELOCITY and DISCHARGE per MINUTE in CIRCULAR SEWERS, with Water flowing at various depths.

Diameter 15 Inches.

Inclination.		One-eighth. (1⅞ Inch.)		One-quarter. (3¾ Inches.)		One-half. (7½ Inches.)		Seven-eighths. (Maximum Discharge.)		Quantity required to give Velocity of 150 Feet per Minute.
	feet per mile	Velocity.	Discharge.	Velocity.	Discharge.	Velocity.	Discharge.	Velocity.	Discharge.	
		feet	gallons	feet	gallons	feet	gallons	feet	gallons	gallons
1 in 40	132	278	150	385	592	500	1900	547	3900	
1 „ 50	105·6	250	135	342	526	446	1700	488	3480	··
1 „ 66	80	218	117	299	460	386	1470	426	3030	··
1 „ 80	66	196	105	272	418	352	1340	386	2750	35
1 „ 100	52·8	176	94	242	372	316	1204	346	2460	50
1 „ 132	40	153	82	211	325	274	1044	301	2140	76
1 „ 165	32	137	73	189	291	245	933	268	1910	106
1 „ 200	26·4	125	67	171	263	223	888	244	1737	146
1 „ 264	20	109	58	149	229	193	735	213	1516	225
1 „ 330	16	97	52	134	206	174	662	190	1350	330
1 „ 440	12	83	44	115	177	150	571	165	1175	567
1 „ 528	10	76	41	105	162	137	520	150	1068	··
1 „ 660	8	68	36	95	146	123	468	134	954	··
1 „ 880	6	60	32	82	126	105	400	116	824	··

Depth of Flow in Proportion to Height of Sewer.

VELOCITY and DISCHARGE per MINUTE in CIRCULAR SEWERS, with Water flowing at various depths.

Diameter 18 Inches.

Inclination.		One-eighth. (2¼ Inches.)		One-quarter. (4½ Inches.)		Depth of Flow in Proportion to Height of Sewer. One-half. (9 Inches.)		Seven-eighths. (Maximum Discharge.)		Quantity required to give Velocity of 150 Feet per Minute.
	feet per mile	Velocity.	Discharge.	Velocity.	Discharge.	Velocity.	Discharge.	Velocity.	Discharge.	
		feet	gallons	feet	gallons	feet	gallons	feet	gallons	gallons
1 in 50	105·6	270	210	382	830	488	2684	536	5500	..
1 ,, 66	80	234	182	326	684	426	2380	466	4776	..
1 ,, 80	66	213	164	290	625	386	2120	423	4336	38
1 ,, 100	52·8	190	147	265	573	346	1903	379	3885	54
1 ,, 132	40	166	129	230	497	301	1655	330	3382	83
1 ,, 165	32	148	115	208	450	268	1474	295	3024	116
1 ,, 200	26·4	135	105	191	414	244	1342	268	2747	157
1 ,, 264	20	117	91	163	340	213	1171	233	2388	243
1 ,, 330	16	105	81	145	312	190	1046	209	2140	353
1 ,, 440	12	91	70	126	272	165	907	180	1845	580
1 ,, 528	10	82	63	116	260	150	825	165	1691	807
1 ,, 660	8	73	57	104	225	135	740	147	1507	..
1 ,, 880	6	65	50	89	192	116	640	127	1302	..
1 ,,1056	5	58	45	81	170	106	585	116	1190	..

c 2

VELOCITY and DISCHARGE per MINUTE in CIRCULAR SEWERS, with Water flowing at various depths.

Diameter 1 Foot 9 Inches.

Inclination.		Depth of Flow in Proportion to Height of Sewer.								Quantity required to give Velocity of 150 Feet per Minute.
		One-eighth. (2¼ Inches.)		One-quarter. (5¼ Inches.)		One-half. (10½ Inches.)		Seven-eighths. (Maximum Discharge.)		
	feet per mile	Velocity.	Discharge.	Velocity.	Discharge.	Velocity.	Discharge.	Velocity.	Discharge.	
		feet	gallons	feet	gallons	feet	gallons	feet	gallons	gallons
1 in 50	105·6	292	306	406	1200	524	3930	582	8150	..
1 " 66	80	254	266	354	1050	456	3420	506	7080	..
1 " 80	66	230	241	322	950	414	3115	460	6440	42
1 " 100	52·8	206	216	288	849	370	2775	411	5754	58
1 " 132	40	179	188	251	740	322	2415	358	5012	89
1 " 165	32	160	168	224	661	288	2160	320	4480	125
1 " 200	26·4	146	153	203	599	262	1965	291	4074	167
1 " 264	20	127	133	177	524	228	1710	253	3542	257
1 " 330	16	113	119	158	462	204	1530	226	3162	375
1 " 440	12	98	103	137	404	176	1320	196	2744	600
1 " 528	10	89	94	125	369	161	1207	179	2506	830
1 " 660	8	80	84	112	330	144	1080	160	2240	1270
1 " 880	6	69	72	97	286	125	937	138	1932	..
1 " 1056	5	63	66	89	263	114	855	126	1770	..

VELOCITY and DISCHARGE per MINUTE in CIRCULAR SEWERS, with Water flowing at various depths.

Diameter 2 Feet.

	Depth of Flow in Proportion to Height of Sewer.								
Inclination.	One-eighth (3 Inches.)		One-quarter (6 Inches.)		One-half (1 Foot.)		Seven-eighths (Maximum Discharge.)		Quantity required to give Velocity of 150 Feet per Minute.
	Velocity.	Discharge.	Velocity.	Discharge.	Velocity.	Discharge.	Velocity.	Discharge.	
	feet per mile	feet	gallons	feet	gallons	feet	gallons	feet	gallons	gallons
1 in 66	80	270	370	378	1450	492	4820	538	9800	.
1 ,, 80	66	246	338	344	1324	446	4370	490	8820	45
1 ,, 100	52·8	220	301	307	1182	398	3900	438	8000	62
1 ,, 132	40	191	262	284	1092	348	3410	381	6950	9¼
1 ,, 165	32	171	234	239	920	311	3048	340	6200	133
1 ,, 200	26·4	155	212	217	835	282	2764	309	5640	177
1 ,, 264	20	135	185	189	728	246	2411	269	4900	274
1 ,, 330	18	121	166	169	650	220	2156	241	4400	397
1 ,, 440	12	105	145	146	562	190	1862	208	3800	630
1 ,, 528	10	96	131	134	515	174	1705	190	3470	850
1 ,, 660	8	85	116	119	458	155	1519	170	3100	1300
1 ,, 880	6	74	101	103	396	134	1313	148	2700	..
1 ,, 1056	5	68	93	95	366	123	1205	134	2485	..
1 ,, 1320	4	60	82	84	323	110	1078	120	2200	..

VELOCITY and DISCHARGE per MINUTE in CIRCULAR SEWERS, with Water flowing at various depths.

Diameter 2 Feet 3 Inches.

Inclination		Depth of Flow in Proportion to Height of Sewer.								Quantity required to give Velocity of 150 Feet per Minute.
		One-eighth. (3¾ Inch.)		One-quarter. (6¾ Inches.)		One-half. (1 Foot 1¼ Inch.)		Seven-eighths. (Maximum Discharge.)		
	feet per mile	Velocity.	Discharge.	Velocity.	Discharge.	Velocity.	Discharge.	Velocity.	Discharge.	
		feet	gallons	feet	gallons	feet	gallons	feet	gallons	gallons
1 in 66	80	286	500	400	1950	520	6420	570	13,180	..
1 ,, 80	66	261	450	361	1772	473	5830	520	11,900	48
1 ,, 100	52·8	232	403	326	1587	423	5220	464	10,728	66
1 ,, 132	40	203	353	284	1383	368	4541	404	9,340	101
1 ,, 165	32	181	314	253	1232	329	4060	361	8,346	141
1 ,, 200	26·4	165	287	230	1120	298	3677	328	7,583	187
1 ,, 264	20	143	248	200	974	260	3205	285	6,589	289
1 ,, 330	16	128	222	179	872	233	2875	255	5,895	419
1 ,, 440	12	111	193	155	755	201	2480	221	5,109	660
1 ,, 528	10	102	177	142	691	184	2270	202	4,670	880
1 ,, 660	8	92	160	126	614	164	2024	180	4,162	1340
1 ,, 880	6	78	135	109	531	142	1752	157	3,620	2250
1 ,, 1056	5	71	123	100	487	130	1604	143	3,300	..
1 ,, 1320	4	64	111	89	433	116	1431	128	2,959	..

VELOCITY and DISCHARGE per MINUTE in CIRCULAR SEWERS, with Water flowing at various depths.

Diameter 2 Feet 6 Inches.

Inclination.		Depth of Flow in Proportion to Height of Sewer.								Quantity required to give Velocity of 150 Feet per Minute.
		One-eighth. (3¾ Inches.)		One-quarter. (7½ Inches.)		One-half. (1 Foot 3 Inches.)		Seven-eighths. (Maximum Discharge.)		
	feet per mile	Velocity.	Discharge.	Velocity.	Discharge.	Velocity.	Discharge.	Velocity.	Discharge.	
		feet	gallons	feet	gallons	feet	gallons	feet	gallons	gallons
1 in 66	80	302	650	422	2520	550	8420	602	17,150	42
1 ,, 100	52·8	246	529	344	2067	447	6843	486	13,851	70
1 ,, 132	40	214	460	299	1797	389	5955	426	12,141	106
1 ,, 165	32	191	411	267	1505	347	5312	381	10,858	148
1 ,, 200	26·4	174	374	243	1460	315	4823	345	9,832	197
1 ,, 264	20	151	325	211	1268	275	4210	301	8,578	303
1 ,, 330	16	135	290	189	1136	246	3766	269	7,666	430
1 ,, 440	12	117	251	164	986	213	3261	233	6,640	690
1 ,, 528	10	107	230	150	901	194	2970	213	6,070	900
1 ,, 660	8	96	206	134	805	174	2664	190	5,415	1380
1 ,, 880	6	82	176	115	691	150	2296	165	4,702	2270
1 ,, 1056	5	75	161	105	631	137	2097	150	4,275	3500
1 ,, 1320	4	68	146	94	565	123	1883	134	3,819	..
1 ,, 1760	3	58	125	82	493	106	1630	116	3,320	..

VELOCITY and DISCHARGE per MINUTE in CIRCULAR SEWERS, with Water flowing at various depths.

Diameter 2 Feet 9 Inches.

Inclination. (feet per mile)	One-eighth. (4½ Inches.)		One-quarter. (8¼ In.hes.)		One-half. (1 Foot 4½ Inches.)		Seven-eighths. (Maximum Discharge.)		Quantity required to give Velocity of 150 Feet per Minute.
	Velocity.	Discharge.	Velocity.	Discharge.	Velocity.	Discharge.	Velocity.	Discharge.	
	feet	gallons	feet	gallons	feet	gallons	feet	gallons	gallons
1 in 66 — 80	316	822	444	3232	570	10,675	632	21,800	..
1 " 100 — 52·8	258	671	360	2621	469	8,690	513	17,698	74
1 " 132 — 40	224	582	313	2279	407	7,542	447	15,420	111
1 " 165 — 32	200	520	280	2038	365	6,763	399	13,765	155
1 " 200 — 26·4	183	476	255	1856	331	6,133	363	12,523	207
1 " 264 — 20	158	411	222	1616	288	5,337	316	10,902	316
1 " 330 — 16	142	369	198	1441	258	4,781	282	9,729	450
1 " 440 — 12	124	322	172	1252	223	4,132	244	8,418	713
1 " 528 — 10	112	291	157	1143	203	3,761	223	7,693	940
1 " 660 — 8	100	260	140	1019	182	3,374	200	6,900	1420
1 " 880 — 6	87	226	121	881	158	2,928	173	5,970	2300
1 " 1056 — 5	79	207	110	801	144	2,668	158	5,450	3300
1 " 1320 — 4	71	185	99	753	129	2,390	141	4,864	..
1 " 1760 — 3	62	166	86	626	111	2,060	122	4,210	..

Depth of Flow in Proportion to Height of Sewer.

VELOCITY and DISCHARGE per MINUTE in CIRCULAR SEWERS, with Water flowing at various depths.

Diameter 3 Feet.

Inclination.		Depth of Flow in Proportion to Height of Sewer.								Quantity required to give Velocity of 150 Feet per Minute.
		One-eighth. (4½ Inches.)		One-quarter. (9 Inches.)		One-half. (1 Foot 6 Inches.)		Seven-eighths. (Maximum Discharge.)		
	feet per mile	Velocity.	Discharge.	Velocity.	Discharge.	Velocity.	Discharge.	Velocity.	Discharge.	
		feet	gallons	feet	gallons	feet	gallons	feet	gallons	gallons
1 in 66	80	332	1027	462	3999	604	13,290	660	27,100	··
1 ,, 100	52·8	269	832	376	3255	489	10,760	534	21,926	78
1 ,, 132	40	235	727	328	2839	426	9,370	464	19,052	116
1 ,, 165	32	210	650	284	2458	380	8,360	416	17,080	162
1 ,, 200	26·4	190	588	266	2302	346	7,610	380	15,603	217
1 ,, 264	20	166	514	231	1999	302	6,640	330	13,550	329
1 ,, 330	16	148	458	207	1792	268	5,900	296	12,154	468
1 ,, 440	12	128	396	179	1549	230	5,060	256	10,500	738
1 ,, 528	10	117	363	164	1419	212	4,660	232	9,526	1000
1 ,, 660	8	104	322	146	1264	190	4,180	208	8,540	1460
1 ,, 880	6	91	281	126	1091	165	3,630	181	7,432	2330
1 ,, 1056	5	83	257	115	995	151	3,320	165	6,774	3300
1 ,, 1320	4	74	229	103	891	134	2,950	148	6,055	··
1 ,, 1760	3	64	198	89	770	115	2,530	128	5,255	··

VELOCITY and DISCHARGE per MINUTE in CIRCULAR SEWERS, with Water flowing at various depths.

Diameter 3 Feet 6 Inches.

Inclination.		Depth of Flow in Proportion to Height of Sewer.								Quantity required to give Velocity of 150 Feet per Minute.
		One-eighth. (5¼ Inches.)		One-quarter. (10½ Inches.)		One-half. (1 Foot 9 Inches.)		Seven-eighths. (Maximum Discharge.)		
		Velocity.	Discharge.	Velocity.	Discharge.	Velocity.	Discharge.	Velocity.	Discharge.	
	feet per mile	feet	gallons	feet	gallons	feet	gallons	feet	gallons	gallons
1 in 66	80	359	1508	501	5887	651	19,530	713	39,860	..
1 „ 132	40	253	1002	355	4171	460	13,800	604	28,200	126
1 „ 200	26·4	206	865	288	3384	374	11,220	404	22,600	235
1 „ 264	20	179	752	251	2949	325	9,750	356	19,930	345
1 „ 330	16	160	672	224	2632	291	8,730	319	17,850	504
1 „ 440	12	139	584	194	2279	252	7,560	276	15,430	790
1 „ 528	10	126	529	177	2080	230	6,900	252	14,100	1045
1 „ 660	8	113	475	158	1856	206	6,180	225	12,590	1500
1 „ 880	6	98	412	136	1598	178	5,340	195	10,900	2430
1 „ 1056	5	90	378	125	1469	162	4,860	178	9,960	3360
1 „ 1320	4	80	336	112	1316	145	4,350	159	8,900	5080
1 „ 1760	3	69	290	97	1140	126	3,780	138	7,720	..
1 „ 2112	2·5	63	265	88	1040	115	3,450	126	7,050	..
1 „ 2640	2	56	235	79	930	103	3,090	113	6,320	..

VELOCITY and DISCHARGE per MINUTE in CIRCULAR SEWERS, with Water flowing at various depths.

Diameter 4 Feet.

Inclination.	One-eighth. (6 Inches.)		One-quarter. (1 Foot.)		One-half. (2 Feet.)		Seven-eighths. (Maximum Discharge.)		Quantity required to give Velocity of 150 Feet per Minute.
feet per mile	Velocity.	Discharge.	Velocity.	Discharge.	Velocity.	Discharge.	Velocity.	Discharge.	
	feet	gallons	feet	gallons	feet	gallons	feet	gallons	gallons
1 in 66 — 80	384	2110	536	8240	695	27,240	764	55,780	..
1 ,, 132 — 40	271	1490	372	5720	492	19,300	539	39,340	..
1 ,, 200 — 26·4	220	1210	302	4640	400	15,680	438	31,970	245
1 ,, 264 — 20	192	1055	268	4120	348	13,640	382	27,890	375
1 ,, 330 — 16	171	940	238	3658	310	12,150	340	24,820	535
1 ,, 440 — 12	148	814	204	3136	269	10,540	294	21,460	830
1 ,, 528 — 10	134	737	186	2860	246	9,650	269	19,650	1100
1 ,, 660 — 8	121	665	166	2550	220	8,620	241	17,600	1580
1 ,, 880 — 6	105	577	146	2244	190	7,450	208	15,180	2530
1 ,, 1056 — 5	96	528	134	2059	174	6,820	191	13,940	3500
1 ,, 1320 — 4	86	473	119	1829	155	6,075	170	12,410	5100
1 ,, 1760 — 3	74	407	102	1568	134	5,260	147	10,730	..
1 ,, 2112 — 2·5	67	368	93	1430	123	4,825	135	9,830	..
1 ,, 2640 — 2	60	330	83	1275	110	4,310	121	8,800	..

VELOCITY and DISCHARGE per MINUTE in CIRCULAR SEWERS, with Water flowing at various depths.

Diameter 5 Feet.

| Inclination | | Depth of Flow in Proportion to Height of Sewer. | | | | | | | | Quantity required to give Velocity of 150 Feet per Minute. |
| | | One-eighth. (7¼ Inches.) | | One-quarter. (1 Foot 3 Inches.) | | One-half. (2 Feet 6 Inches.) | | Seven-eighths. (Maximum Discharge.) | | |
	feet per mile	Velocity.	Discharge.	Velocity.	Discharge.	Velocity.	Discharge.	Velocity.	Discharge.	
		feet	gallons	feet	gallons	feet	gallons	feet	gallons	gallons
1 in 66	80	428	3680	600	14,400	776	47,300	852	97,180	..
1 „ 132	40	302	2600	422	10,150	548	33,400	602	68,640	..
1 „ 200	26·4	246	2115	342	8,220	446	27,180	488	55,630	..
1 „ 284	20	214	1840	300	7,200	388	23,650	426	48,590	420
1 „ 330	16	194	1670	268	6,430	348	21,210	380	43,320	590
1 „ 440	12	166	1430	230	5,530	300	18,280	330	37,620	920
1 „ 528	10	151	1300	211	5,075	274	16,700	301	34,320	1,220
1 „ 660	8	136	1170	189	4,540	246	15,000	268	30,550	1,730
1 „ 880	6	117	1000	164	3,945	213	12,980	232	26,450	2,800
1 „ 1056	5	107	920	150	3,600	194	11,820	213	24,300	3,600
1 „ 1320	4	97	835	134	3,215	174	10,600	190	21,660	5,380
1 „ 1760	3	83	715	115	2,705	150	9,140	165	18,860	9,040
1 „ 2112	2·5	75	650	105	2,540	137	8,350	151	17,160	12,800
1 „ 2640	2	68	585	90	2,270	123	7,500	134	15,275	..

VELOCITY and DISCHARGE per MINUTE in CIRCULAR SEWERS, with Water flowing at various depths.

Diameter 6 Feet.

Inclination	feet per mile	Depth of Flow in Proportion to Height of Sewer.								Quantity required to give Velocity of 150 Feet per Minute.
		One-eighth. (9 Inches.)		One-quarter. (1 Foot 6 Inches.)		One-half. (3 Feet.)		Seven-eighths. (Maximum Discharge.)		
		Velocity.	Discharge.	Velocity.	Discharge.	Velocity.	Discharge.	Velocity.	Discharge.	
		feet	gallons	feet	gallons	feet	gallons	feet	gallons	gallons
1 in 66	80	468	5790	652	22,580	852	75,200	932	153,000	..
1 „ 132	40	332	4110	462	16,000	602	53,120	660	108,400	..
1 „ 200	26·4	270	3340	382	13,140	488	43,060	536	88,040	..
1 „ 264	20	234	2895	326	11,290	426	37,600	466	76,500	455
1 „ 330	16	210	2610	290	10,040	380	33,535	418	68,660	640
1 „ 440	12	182	2250	252	8,720	330	29,120	380	59,130	980
1 „ 528	10	166	2055	232	8,000	301	26,560	330	54,200	1,320
1 „ 660	8	148	1830	208	7,200	270	23,830	294	48,290	1,890
1 „ 880	6	129	1600	178	6,160	232	20,480	254	41,740	2,950
1 „ 1056	5	117	1448	162	5,645	212	18,800	233	38,250	3,850
1 „ 1320	4	105	1300	145	5,020	190	16,770	209	34,330	5,670
1 „ 1760	3	91	1126	126	4,360	165	14,560	180	29,560	9,340
1 „ 2112	2·5	83	1027	116	4,000	150	13,280	165	27,100	13,200
2 „ 2640	2	74	917	104	3,600	135	11,915	147	24,140	..

TABLE VI.—VELOCITY and DISCHARGE per MINUTE in EGG-SHAPED SEWERS, with Water flowing at various depths.

Sewer 2 Feet × 1 Foot 4 Inches.

Inclination		Depth of Flow in Proportion to Height of Sewer.								Quantity required to give Velocity of 150 Feet per Minute.
		One-eighth. (3 Inches.)		One-quarter. (6 Inches.)		One-half. (1 Foot.)		Seven-eighths. (Maximum Discharge.)		
	feet per mile	Velocity.	Discharge.	Velocity.	Discharge.	Velocity.	Discharge.	Velocity.	Discharge.	
		feet	gallons	feet	gallons	feet	gallons	feet	gallons	gallons
1 in 50	105·6	295	223	380	790	480	2720	595	6910	..
1 ,, 66	80	257	196	331	686	417	2360	468	5440	..
1 ,, 100	52·8	210	160	268	556	339	1921	381	4430	38
1 ,, 132	40	183	139	234	486	295	1674	331	3850	60
1 ,, 165	32	163	124	210	436	264	1496	297	3450	80
1 ,, 200	26·4	148	112	190	395	240	1360	270	3138	120
1 ,, 264	20	129	98	166	346	208	1180	234	2720	210
1 ,, 330	16	116	88	148	305	186	1056	210	2440	330
1 ,, 440	12	99	76	128	268	162	918	182	2115	620
1 ,, 528	10	91	69	117	243	148	838	166	1925	920
1 ,, 660	8	81	62	105	216	132	748	148	1725	:
1 ,, 880	6	70	53	91	189	114	616	120	1490	:
1 ,, 1056	5	64	47	83	172	104	590	117	1360	:
1 ,, 1320	4	58	44	74	153	93	527	105	1220	:

VELOCITY and DISCHARGE per MINUTE in EGG-SHAPED SEWERS, with Water flowing at various depths.

Sewer 2 Feet 3 Inches × 1 Foot 6 Inches.

Inclination		One-eighth. (3⅜ Inches.)		One-quarter. (6¾ Inches.)		One-half. (1 Foot 1½ Inch.)		Seven-eighths. (Maximum Discharge.)		Quantity required to give Velocity of 150 Feet per Minute.
	feet per mile	Velocity.	Discharge.	Velocity.	Discharge.	Velocity.	Discharge.	Velocity.	Discharge.	
		feet	gallons	feet	gallons	feet	gallons	feet	gallons	gallons
1 in 50	105·6	312	300	402	1054	508	4180	572	8400	..
1 " 66	80	271	260	350	920	443	3900	497	7310	..
1 " 100	52·8	221	212	285	747	360	3175	404	5940	41
1 " 132	40	192	185	248	650	314	2770	352	5180	63
1 " 165	32	172	167	222	582	280	2470	314	4620	85
1 " 200	26·4	156	150	201	527	254	2240	286	4200	120
1 " 264	20	135	130	176	460	222	1960	248	3650	210
1 " 330	16	121	116	156	409	198	1750	222	3265	330
1 " 440	12	105	101	136	356	172	1512	192	2824	610
1 " 528	10	97	93	124	325	156	1380	176	2590	900
1 " 660	8	86	83	111	290	140	1235	157	2310	2000
1 " 880	6	74	71	96	250	121	1067	126	2000	..
1 " 1056	5	68	65	88	230	111	980	124	1824	..
1 " 1320	4	61	59	78	204	99	874	111	1688	..

VELOCITY and DISCHARGE per MINUTE in EGG-SHAPED SEWERS, with Water flowing at various depths.

Sewer 2 Feet 6 Inches × 1 Foot 10 Inches.

Inclination		One-eighth. (3¼ Inches.)		One-quarter. (7¼ Inches.)		One-half. (1 Foot 3 Inches.)		Seven-eighths. (Maximum Discharge.)		Quantity required to give Velocity of 150 Feet per Minute.
	feet per mile	Velocity.	Discharge.	Velocity.	Discharge.	Velocity.	Discharge.	Velocity.	Discharge.	
		feet	gallons	feet	gallons	feet	gallons	feet	gallons	gallons
1 in 66	80	280	338	371	1203	467	4138	522	9500	..
1 ,, 100	52·8	220	272	301	972	369	3350	424	7700	43
1 ,, 132	40	193	238	261	846	330	2924	369	6700	65
1 ,, 165	32	176	214	236	764	296	2620	330	6000	90
1 ,, 200	26·4	160	193	212	687	268	2375	300	5460	125
1 ,, 264	20	140	169	186	601	233	2069	261	4750	210
1 ,, 330	16	124	150	165	534	209	1852	235	4280	335
1 ,, 440	12	108	131	143	463	180	1598	202	3670	600
1 ,, 528	10	99	120	131	424	165	1462	185	3350	890
1 ,, 660	8	88	107	118	382	148	1311	165	3000	1500
1 ,, 880	6	77	93	101	328	128	1132	143	2600	..
1 ,, 1056	5	70	84	92	300	117	1034	131	2380	..
1 ,, 1320	4	62	74	82	266	105	926	118	2140	..
1 ,, 1760	3	54	65	71	230	90	800	101	1834	..

Depth of Flow in proportion to Height of Sewer.

VELOCITY and DISCHARGE per MINUTE in EGG-SHAPED SEWERS, with Water flowing at various depths.

Sewer 2 Feet 9 Inches × 1 Foot 10 Inches.

Inclination.		One-eighth. (4¼ Inches.)		One-quarter. (8¼ Inches.)		One-half. (1 Foot 4¼ Inches.)		Seven-eighths. (Maximum Discharge.)		Quantity required to give Velocity of 160 Feet per Minute.
		Velocity.	Discharge.	Velocity.	Discharge.	Velocity.	Discharge.	Velocity.	Discharge.	
	feet per mile	feet	gallons	feet	gallons	feet	gallons	feet	gallons	gallons
1 in 66	80	300	432	387	1518	489	5230	550	12,050	..
1 ,, 100	52·8	243	350	313	1230	402	4300	446	9,800	45
1 ,, 132	40	212	305	274	1077	345	3690	389	8,550	70
1 ,, 165	32	190	274	244	956	308	3300	348	7,720	100
1 ,, 200	26·4	172	248	222	870	284	3040	316	6,950	130
1 ,, 264	20	150	216	194	760	244	2610	274	6,020	215
1 ,, 330	16	134	192	172	674	218	2333	246	5,400	345
1 ,, 440	12	116	168	150	588	190	2033	214	4,700	588
1 ,, 528	10	106	153	137	538	172	1840	194	4,270	880
1 ,, 660	8	95	137	122	478	154	1650	174	3,860	1440
1 ,, 880	6	82	118	106	411	133	1420	150	3,300	3300
1 ,, 1056	5	75	108	97	380	122	1310	137	3,010	..
1 ,, 1320	4	67	96	86	337	109	1166	123	2,700	..
1 ,, 1760	3	58	84	75	294	95	1016	107	2,350	..

D

VELOCITY and DISCHARGE per MINUTE in EGG-SHAPED SEWERS, with Water flowing at various depths.

Sewer 3 Feet × 2 Feet.

Inclination		Depth of Flow in Proportion to Height of Sewer.								Quantity required to give Velocity of 150 Feet per Minute.
	feet per mile	One-eighth. (4½ Inches.)		One-quarter. (9 Inches.)		One-half. (1 Foot 6 Inches.)		Seven-eighths. (Maximum Discharge.)		
		Velocity.	Discharge	Velocity.	Discharge.	Velocity.	Discharge.	Velocity.	Discharge.	gallons
		feet	gallons	feet	gallons	feet	gallons	feet	gallons	
1 in 66	80	313	540	404	1880	510	6500	574	14,900	..
1 „ 100	52·8	255	437	322	1504	414	5280	467	12,120	..
1 „ 132	40	221	380	286	1335	361	4600	407	10,550	75
1 „ 165	32	198	338	256	1200	324	4130	364	9,450	100
1 „ 200	26·4	180	309	228	1064	293	3735	330	8,570	135
1 „ 264	20	157	270	202	940	255	3250	286	7,450	215
1 „ 330	16	139	238	180	840	228	2910	257	6,680	350
1 „ 440	12	121	208	156	728	198	2525	222	5,770	530
1 „ 528	10	111	190	143	668	180	2300	203	5,270	870
1 „ 660	8	99	169	128	600	162	2065	182	4,725	1400
1 „ 880	6	86	147	111	517	140	1785	157	4,075	2800
1 „ 1056	5	78	135	101	470	128	1620	143	3,730	..
1 „ 1320	4	70	120	90	420	114	1455	128	3,340	..
1 „ 1760	3	61	105	78	364	99	1262	111	2,885	..

VELOCITY and DISCHARGE per MINUTE in EGG-SHAPED SEWERS, with Water flowing at various depths.

Sewer 3 Feet 3 Inches × 2 Feet 2 Inches.

Inclination.			Depth of Flow in Proportion to Height of Sewer.								Quantity required to give Velocity of 150 Feet per Minute.
		feet per mile	One-eighth. (4¼ Inches.)		One-quarter. (9¾ Inches.)		One-half. (1 Foot 7¼ Inches.)		Seven-eighths. (Maximum Discharge.)		
			Velocity.	Discharge.	Velocity.	Discharge.	Velocity.	Discharge.	Velocity.	Discharge.	gallons.
			feet	gallons	feet	gallons	feet	gallons	feet	gallons	
1 in	66	80	326	655	421	2300	532	7975	598	18,240	..
,,	100	52·8	264	531	341	1865	432	6475	490	14,935	..
,,	132	40	230	462	298	1630	376	5635	422	12,870	75
,,	165	32	207	416	266	1455	336	5040	378	11,530	100
,,	200	26·4	186	374	241	1320	304	4560	344	10,490	135
,,	264	20	161	324	210	1150	266	3990	299	9,120	220
,,	330	16	143	287	187	1023	238	3565	267	8,140	350
,,	440	12	126	253	164	897	206	3090	232	7,075	590
,,	528	10	115	231	149	825	187	2800	211	6,435	865
,,	660	8	103	207	133	727	168	2520	189	5,765	1390
,,	880	6	89	179	115	630	145	2170	162	4,940	2700
,,	1056	5	81	163	105	574	133	1995	150	4,560	4550
,,	1320	4	71	144	93	511	119	1785	133	4,055	..
,,	1760	3	63	127	82	448	103	1540	116	3,540	..

VELOCITY and DISCHARGE per MINUTE in EGG-SHAPED SEWERS, with Water flowing at various depths.

Sewer 3 Feet 6 Inches × 2 Feet 4 Inches.

Inclination		Depth of Flow in Proportion to Height of Sewer.								Quantity required to give Velocity of 150 Feet per Minute.
		One-eighth. (5¼ Inches.)		One-quarter. (10½ Inches.)		One-half. (1 Foot 9 Inches.)		Seven-eighths. (Maximum Discharge.)		
	feet per mile	Velocity.	Discharge.	Velocity.	Discharge.	Velocity.	Discharge.	Velocity.	Discharge.	
		feet	gallons	feet	gallons	feet	gallons	feet	gallons	gallons
1 in 100	52·8	275	642	355	2260	448	7760	504	17,950	..
1 ,, 132	40	240	560	300	1900	390	6760	440	15,660	80
1 ,, 165	32	214	500	276	1740	350	6000	394	14,030	110
1 ,, 200	26·4	195	455	251	1600	317	5490	357	12,700	140
1 ,, 264	20	170	396	218	1370	275	4780	312	11,100	220
1 ,, 330	16	152	355	196	1240	247	4280	278	9,900	355
1 ,, 440	12	132	308	170	1080	215	3730	242	8,600	600
1 ,, 528	10	120	280	154	950	195	3380	220	7,830	865
1 ,, 660	8	107	250	138	870	175	3000	197	7,015	1380
1 ,, 880	6	93	217	120	760	151	2620	170	6,050	2550
1 ,, 1056	5	85	198	109	690	138	2390	157	5,500	4200
1 ,, 1320	4	76	177	98	623	124	2140	139	4,950	..
1 ,, 1760	3	66	154	85	540	108	1870	121	4,300	..
1 ,, 2640	2	53	124	69	437	87	1500	98	3,510	..

VELOCITY and DISCHARGE per MINUTE in EGG-SHAPED SEWERS, with Water flowing at various depths.

Sewer 3 Feet 9 Inches × 2 Feet 6 Inches.

Inclination		One-eighth (5¼ Inches.)		One-quarter (11¼ Inches.)		One-half (1 Foot 10¼ Inches.)		Seven-eighths (Maximum Discharge.)		Quantity required to give Velocity of 150 Feet per Minute.
		Velocity.	Discharge.	Velocity.	Discharge.	Velocity.	Discharge.	Velocity.	Discharge.	
	feet per mile	feet	gallons	feet	gallons	feet	gallons	feet	gallons	gallons
1 in 100	52·8	284	758	367	2665	464	9190	521	21,200	..
1 ,, 132	40	248	662	319	2315	404	8000	454	18,460	80
1 ,, 165	32	222	592	286	2075	360	7130	405	16,470	115
1 ,, 200	26·4	201	536	260	1890	328	6495	369	15,000	145
1 ,, 264	20	175	467	226	1640	285	5645	321	13,050	225
1 ,, 330	16	157	418	201	1460	255	5050	287	11,670	360
1 ,, 440	12	136	362	175	1270	221	4375	249	10,125	610
1 ,, 528	10	124	331	160	1160	202	4000	227	9,230	865
1 ,, 660	8	111	296	143	1038	180	3565	203	8,240	1350
1 ,, 880	6	96	256	124	901	156	3090	176	7,165	2550
1 ,, 1056	5	87	234	113	820	143	2830	160	6,520	3850
1 ,, 1320	4	78	209	101	730	127	2525	143	5,825	..
1 ,, 1760	3	68	181	87	635	110	2188	124	5,060	..
1 ,, 2640	2	55	148	71	515	90	1782	102	4,120	..

VELOCITY and DISCHARGE per MINUTE in EGG-SHAPED SEWERS, with Water flowing at various depths.

Sewer 4 Feet × 2 Feet 8 Inches.

Inclination		feet per mile	Depth of Flow in Proportion to Height of Sewer.								Quantity required to give Velocity of 150 Feet per Minute.
			One-eighth. (6 Inches.)		One-quarter. (1 Foot.)		One-half. (2 Feet.)		Seven-eighths. (Maximum Discharge.)		
			Velocity.	Discharge.	Velocity.	Discharge.	Velocity.	Discharge.	Velocity.	Discharge.	
			feet	gallons	feet	gallons	feet	gallons	feet	gallons	gallons
1 in 100		52·8	204	884	380	3150	470	10,850	537	25,000	..
1 ,, 132		40	255	780	330	2740	417	9,440	468	21,760	80
1 ,, 165		32	226	680	295	2450	372	8,420	420	19,500	120
1 ,, 200		26·4	203	635	263	2220	339	7,675	380	17,670	150
1 ,, 264		20	181	550	234	1940	295	6,680	332	15,430	225
1 ,, 330		16	162	490	208	1725	264	5,980	297	13,800	360
1 ,, 440		12	140	430	180	1500	228	5,160	256	11,900	610
1 ,, 528		10	128	390	165	1350	208	4,720	234	10,880	860
1 ,, 660		8	113	340	148	1230	186	4,210	210	9,750	1350
1 ,, 880		6	99	300	128	1065	162	3,668	182	8,460	2500
1 ,, 1056		5	90	275	117	970	148	3,340	166	7,720	4000
1 ,, 1320		4	81	245	104	863	132	2,990	148	6,900	..
1 ,, 1760		3	70	210	90	750	114	2,580	128	5,950	..
1 ,, 2640		2	57	170	74	615	93	2,105	105	4,880	..

VELOCITY and DISCHARGE per MINUTE in EGG-SHAPED SEWERS, with Water flowing at various depths.

Sewer 4 Feet 6 Inches × 3 Feet.

Inclination.		One-eighth. (6¾ Inches.)		One-quarter. (1 Foot 1¼ Inch.)		One-half. (2 Feet 3 Inches.)		Seven-eighths. (Maximum Discharge.)		Quantity required to give Velocity of 150 Feet per Minute.
	feet per mile	Velocity.	Discharge.	Velocity.	Discharge.	Velocity.	Discharge.	Velocity.	Discharge.	
		feet	gallons	feet	gallons	feet	gallons	feet	gallons	gallons
1 in 100	52·8	314	1230	402	4300	508	14,540	570	33,500	..
1 ,, 132	40	271	1050	350	3740	442	12,650	497	29,250	85
1 ,, 165	32	240	925	314	3360	396	11,320	444	26,130	125
1 ,, 200	26·4	223	860	284	3040	360	10,300	405	23,830	160
1 ,, 264	20	192	740	248	2655	312	8,930	352	20,720	235
1 ,, 330	16	172	664	222	2375	280	8,000	314	18,480	370
1 ,, 440	12	148	572	192	2055	242	6,920	272	16,000	620
1 ,, 528	10	136	525	175	1870	221	6,325	248	14,600	860
1 ,, 660	8	120	463	157	1680	198	5,660	222	13,060	1350
1 ,, 880	6	105	405	136	1455	171	4,700	192	11,300	2400
1 ,, 1056	5	96	372	124	1330	156	4,465	176	10,360	3550
1 ,, 1320	4	86	334	111	1190	140	4,000	157	9,240	6100
1 ,, 1760	3	74	286	96	1030	121	3,460	138	8,000	..
1 ,, 2640	2	60	232	78	840	99	2,834	111	6,530	..

Depth of Flow in Proportion to Height of Sewer.

VELOCITY and DISCHARGE per MINUTE in EGG-SHAPED SEWERS, with Water flowing at various depths.

Sewers 5 Feet × 3 Feet 4 Inches.

| Inclination | Depth of Flow in Proportion to Height of Sewer. | | | | | | | | Quantity required to give Velocity of 150 Feet per Minute. |
| | One-eighth (1¾ Inches.) | | One-quarter (1 Foot 3 Inches.) | | One-half (2 Feet 6 Inches.) | | Seven-eighths. (Maximum Discharge.) | | |
feet per mile	Velocity.	Discharge.	Velocity.	Discharge.	Velocity.	Discharge.	Velocity.	Discharge.	
	feet	gallons	feet	gallons	feet	gallons	feet	gallons	gallons
1 in 100 — 52·8	322	1554	424	5510	537	19,050	600	43,550	..
1 ,, 132 — 40	280	1342	370	4800	466	16,520	522	37,900	90
1 ,, 165 — 32	252	1205	332	4300	418	14,800	466	33,840	130
1 ,, 200 — 26·4	228	1092	300	3890	380	13,470	424	30,800	165
1 ,, 264 — 20	198	950	260	3370	330	11,700	368	26,800	250
1 ,, 330 — 16	177	848	222	3000	296	10,500	331	24,040	380
1 ,, 440 — 12	154	738	202	2620	255	9,040	286	20,175	630
1 ,, 528 — 10	140	670	185	2400	233	8,260	261	18,950	865
1 ,, 660 — 8	126	603	166	2150	209	7,400	233	18,920	1,360
1 ,, 880 — 6	109	522	143	1855	181	6,420	202	14,670	2,350
1 ,, 1056 — 5	99	475	130	1690	165	5,850	184	13,380	3,500
1 ,, 1320 — 4	89	425	116	1500	148	5,250	166	12,020	5,700
1 ,, 1760 — 3	77	370	101	1310	127	4,500	143	10,390	..
1 ,, 2640 — 2	63	301	83	1075	104	3,700	116	8,466	..

VELOCITY and DISCHARGE per MINUTE in EGG-SHAPED SEWERS, with Water flowing at various depths.

Sewers 6 Feet × 4 Feet.

Inclination.		One-eighth. (9 Inches.)		One-quarter. (1 Foot 6 Inches.)		One-half. (3 Feet.)		Seven-eighths. (Maximum Discharge.)		Quantity required to give Velocity of 150 Feet per Minute.
	feet per mile	Velocity.	Discharge.	Velocity.	Discharge.	Velocity.	Discharge.	Velocity.	Discharge.	
		feet	gallons	feet	gallons	feet	gallons	feet	gallons	gallons
1 in 100	52·8	357	2451	462	8628	583	29,700	654	68,410	..
1 ,, 132	40	313	2148	401	7488	510	25,984	573	59,938	98
1 ,, 165	32	278	1910	360	6720	456	23,230	512	53,560	140
1 ,, 200	26·4	254	1744	327	6106	414	21,093	466	48,746	175
1 ,, 264	20	221	1517	286	5341	360	18,342	405	42,365	270
1 ,, 330	16	198	1359	255	4762	322	16,406	363	37,970	410
1 ,, 440	12	171	1174	221	4127	279	14,215	314	32,800	640
1 ,, 528	10	156	1072	201	3753	255	12,992	286	29,917	875
1 ,, 660	8	139	954	180	3361	228	11,616	256	26,780	1,380
1 ,, 880	6	121	830	156	2913	197	10,037	242	25,314	2,350
1 ,, 1066	5	110	755	143	2670	180	9,171	202	21,130	3,480
1 ,, 1320	4	99	679	127	2372	161	8,203	181	18,933	5,600
1 ,, 1760	3	85	583	110	2054	140	7,130	156	16,318	11,000
1 ,, 2640	2	69	474	90	1681	114	5,800	128	13,389	..

TABLE VII.—DISCHARGE OF PIPES (running full).

NOTE.—The velocity in feet per minute may be ascertained in each case by dividing the discharge by the number of gallons contained in each lineal foot of the pipe as given at the top of the column.

Ratio of Head of Water to Length of Pipe.	⅜ Inch. (·005 Galls. per Ft.)	½ Inch. (·008 Galls. per Ft.)	¾ Inch. (·019 Galls. per Ft.)	1 Inch. (·034 Galls. per Ft.)	1¼ Inch. (·053 Galls. per Ft.)	1½ Inch. (·076 Galls. per Ft.)	2 Inches. (·135 Galls. per Ft.)	2½ Inches. (·212 Galls. per Ft.)
	galls. per min.	galls. per min.	galls. per min.	galls. per min.	galls. per min.	galls. per min.	galls. per min.	galls. per min.
1 to 1	2·39	4·91	13·52	27·75	48·55	76·66	157·2	274·8
1 " 2	1·70	3·47	9·56	19·63	34·32	54·23	111·2	194·4
1 " 3	1·38	2·85	7·86	16·13	28·20	44·54	91·3	159·7
1 " 4	1·19	2·46	6·76	13·87	24·27	38·33	78·6	137·4
1 " 5	1·07	2·20	6·05	12·40	21·70	34·28	70·3	122·8
1 " 6	·97	2·00	5·52	11·33	19·81	31·29	64·2	112·2
1 " 7	·90	1·85	5·10	10·47	18·32	28·93	59·3	103·7
1 " 8	·85	1·73	4·78	9·81	17·15	27·09	55·5	97·1
1 " 9	·80	1·64	4·51	9·25	16·18	25·55	52·4	91·6
1 " 10	·75	1·55	4·28	8·78	15·36	24·26	49·7	87·0
1 " 12	·69	1·42	3·91	8·02	14·30	22·16	45·4	79·4
1 " 14	·64	1·32	3·62	7·44	13·00	20·50	42·1	73·5
1 " 16	·60	1·23	3·38	6·94	12·14	19·16	39·3	68·7
1 " 18	·56	1·17	3·19	6·53	11·44	18·10	37·1	64·8
1 " 20	·53	1·10	3·03	6·21	10·85	17·15	35·2	61·3

DISCHARGE of PIPES (running full).

NOTE.—The velocity in feet per minute may be ascertained in each case by dividing the discharge by the number of gallons contained in each lineal foot of the pipe as given at the top of the column.

Ratio of Head of Water to Length of Pipe.	⅜ Inch. (·005 Galls. per Ft.)	½ Inch. (·008 Galls. per Ft.)	¾ Inch. (·019 Galls. per Ft.)	1 Inch. (·034 Galls. per Ft.)	1¼ Inch. (·053 Galls. per Ft.)	1½ Inch. (·076 Galls. per Ft.)	2 Inches. (·135 Galls. per Ft.)	2½ Inches. (·212 Galls. per Ft.)
	galls. per min.	galls. per min.	galls. per min.	galls. per min.	galls. per min.	galls. per min.	galls. per min.	galls. per min.
1 to 25	·48	·98	2·71	5·55	9·70	15·33	31·4	55·0
1 „ 30	·44	·90	2·48	5·08	8·90	14·05	29·3	50·0
1 „ 35	·40	·83	2·28	4·69	8·20	12·95	26·5	46·4
1 „ 40	·38	·78	2·14	4·40	7·70	12·12	24·9	43·4
1 „ 45	·36	·73	2·02	4·14	7·23	11·42	23·4	41·0
1 „ 50	·33	·69	1·92	3·93	6·86	10·80	22·2	38·9
1 „ 60	·31	·64	1·76	3·60	6·30	9·90	20·4	35·6
1 „ 70	·28	·59	1·62	3·32	5·80	9·16	18·8	32·8
1 „ 80	·27	·55	1·50	3·10	5·40	8·60	17·5	30·7
1 „ 100	·24	·49	1·34	2·77	4·86	7·66	15·7	27·5
1 „ 120	·21	·44	1·23	2·52	4·40	6·95	14·3	24·9
1 „ 150	·19	·40	1·11	2·27	3·96	6·26	12·8	22·4
1 „ 200	·17	·35	·96	1·96	3·43	5·42	11·1	19·4
1 „ 250	·15	·31	·85	1·75	3·07	4·85	9·9	17·4
1 „ 300	·14	·29	·79	1·61	2·82	4·45	9·1	16·0

Diameter of Pipe.

DISCHARGE OF PIPES (running full).

NOTE.—The velocity in feet per minute may be ascertained in each case by dividing the discharge by the number of gallons contained in each lineal foot of the pipe as given at the top of the column.

Diameter of Pipe.

Ratio of Head of Water to Length of Pipe.	3 Inches. (·305 Galls. per Ft.)	4 Inches. (·54 Galls. per Ft.)	5 Inches. (·85 Galls. per Ft.)	6 Inches. (1·22 Galls. per Ft.)	7 Inches. (1·66 Galls. per Ft.)	8 Inches. (2·17 Galls. per Ft.)	9 Inches. (2·75 Galls. per Ft.)	10 Inches. (3·39 Galls. per Ft.)
	galls. per min.	galls. per min.	galls. per min.	galls. per min.	galls. per min.	galls. per min.	galls. per min.	galls. per min.
1 to 5	193	398	695	1097	1613	2253	3020	3933
1 ,, 10	137	281	491	776	1140	1592	2138	2780
1 ,, 15	112	230	401	633	931	1300	1745	2270
1 ,, 20	97	199	347	548	806	1126	1511	1967
1 ,, 25	86	178	311	491	721	1007	1352	1759
1 ,, 30	79	162	283	448	658	920	1234	1606
1 ,, 35	73	150	263	415	610	851	1142	1487
1 ,, 40	68	141	246	388	570	796	1069	1391
1 ,, 45	64	133	232	366	538	751	1007	1311
1 ,, 50	61	126	222	347	510	712	956	1244
1 ,, 60	56	115	201	317	466	650	873	1136
1 ,, 70	52	106	186	293	431	594	808	1051
1 ,, 80	49	99	174	274	403	563	756	983
1 ,, 90	46	94	164	258	380	536	712	927
1 ,, 100	43	89	155	245	360	503	676	879

DISCHARGE OF PIPES (running full).

NOTE.—The velocity in feet per minute may be ascertained in each case by dividing the discharge by the number of gallons contained in each lineal foot of the pipe as given at the top of the column.

Ratio of Head of Water to Length of Pipe.	Diameter of Pipe.							
	3 Inches. (·305 Galls. per Ft.)	4 Inches. (·54 Galls. per Ft.)	5 Inches. (·85 Galls. per Ft.)	6 Inches. (1·22 Galls. per Ft.)	7 Inches. (1·66 Galls. per Ft.)	8 Inches. (2·17 Galls. per Ft.)	9 Inches. (2·75 Galls. per Ft.)	10 Inches. (3·39 Galls. per Ft.)
	galls. per min.	galls. per min.	galls. per min.	galls. per min.	galls. per min.	galls. per min.	galls. per min.	galls. per min.
1 „ 125	39	80	139	219	323	450	605	786
1 „ 150	36	73	127	200	296	411	552	718
1 „ 175	33	67	117	183	273	380	510	665
1 „ 200	31	62	109	173	262	352	478	622
1 „ 250	27	56	98	154	227	317	426	554
1 „ 300	25	51	90	142	208	291	390	508
1 „ 350	23	47	83	131	193	270	361	470
1 „ 400	21	44	78	123	180	252	338	440
1 „ 450	20	42	73	116	170	238	319	415
1 „ 500	19	40	69	110	161	225	302	393
1 „ 600	18	36	63	100	147	206	276	360
1 „ 700	17	34	59	93	136	191	256	332
1 „ 800	16	31	55	87	127	178	239	320
1 „ 900	15	29	52	82	120	168	226	293
1 „1000	14	28	49	78	114	159	214	278

DISCHARGE OF PIPES (running full).

NOTE.—The velocity in feet per minute may be ascertained in each case by dividing the discharge by the number of gallons contained in each lineal foot of the pipe as given at the top of the column.

Diameter of Pipe.

Ratio of Head of Water to Length of Pipe.	12 Inches. (4·91 Galls. per Ft.)	15 Inches. (7·67 Galls. per Ft.)	18 Inches. (11·04 Galls. per Ft.)	21 Inches. (15 Galls. per Ft.)	24 Inches. (19·6 Galls. per Ft.)	27 Inches. (24·8 Galls. per Ft.)	30 Inches. (30·7 Galls. per Ft.)	36 Inches. (44·2 Galls. per Ft.)
	galls. per min.	galls. per min.	galls. per min.	galls. per min.	galls. per min.	galls. per min.	galls. per min.	galls. per min.
1 to 20	3,103	5,420	8,551	12,570	17,552	23,360	30,660	48,365
1 ,, 25	2,775	4,848	7,648	11,240	15,698	21,070	27,422	43,265
1 ,, 30	2,533	4,426	6,982	10,262	14,330	19,235	25,034	39,490
1 ,, 40	2,194	3,833	6,047	8,888	12,411	16,660	21,680	34,200
1 ,, 50	1,962	3,428	5,408	7,950	11,100	14,900	19,390	30,588
1 ,, 60	1,792	3,130	4,937	7,257	10,133	13,600	17,704	27,926
1 ,, 70	1,660	2,897	4,571	6,717	9,382	12,503	16,390	25,854
1 ,, 80	1,551	2,710	4,276	6,284	8,776	11,943	15,330	24,182
1 ,, 90	1,462	2,555	4,032	5,925	8,274	11,105	14,452	22,000
1 ,, 100	1,387	2,424	3,824	5,621	7,850	10,535	13,712	21,628
1 ,, 125	1,241	2,168	3,420	5,027	7,021	9,423	12,264	19,346
1 ,, 150	1,133	1,980	3,123	4,591	6,411	8,605	11,200	17,665
1 ,, 175	1,049	1,832	2,890	4,250	5,933	7,964	10,365	16,350
1 ,, 200	981	1,714	2,698	3,974	5,538	7,450	9,695	15,294
1 ,, 250	874	1,527	2,410	3,542	4,946	6,638	8,640	13,628

DISCHARGE of PIPES (running full).

NOTE.—The velocity in feet per minute may be ascertained in each case by dividing the discharge by the number of gallons contained in each lineal foot of the pipe as given at the top of the column.

Ratio of Head of Water to Length of Pipe.	12 Inches. (4·91 Galls. per Ft.)	15 Inches. (7·67 Galls. per Ft.)	18 Inches. 11·04 Galls. per Ft.)	21 Inches. (15 Galls. per Ft.)	24 Inches. (19·6 Galls. per Ft.)	27 Inches. (24·8 Galls. per Ft.)	30 Inches. (30·7 Galls. per Ft.)	36 Inches. (44·2 Galls. per Ft.)
	galls. per min.	galls. per min.	galls. per min.	galls. per min.	galls. per min.	galls. per min.	galls. per min.	galls. per min.
1 to 300	801	1,400	2,208	3,245	4,532	6,083	7,916	12,488
1 ,, 350	742	1,296	2,044	3,004	4,196	5,567	7,330	11,560
1 ,, 400	694	1,212	1,912	2,810	3,925	5,268	6,856	10,814
1 ,, 450	654	1,143	1,803	2,650	3,700	4,966	6,464	10,198
1 ,, 500	620	1,084	1,710	2,514	3,510	4,712	6,132	9,675
1 ,, 600	566	990	1,561	2,295	3,204	4,300	5,597	8,830
1 ,, 700	524	916	1,445	2,124	2,971	3,982	5,182	8,174
1 ,, 800	490	857	1,352	1,987	2,775	3,725	4,848	7,647
1 ,, 900	462	808	1,275	1,873	2,616	3,512	4,570	7,240
1 ,, 1000	439	766	1,210	1,777	2,482	3,332	4,336	6,840
1 ,, 1250	392	684	1,081	1,590	2,220	2,980	3,878	6,118
1 ,, 1500	358	627	987	1,451	2,027	2,720	3,540	5,585
1 ,, 2000	310	542	855	1,257	1,755	2,356	3,066	4,836
1 ,, 3000	253	443	698	1,026	1,433	1,924	2,503	3,949
1 ,, 5000	196	343	541	795	1,110	1,490	1,939	3,059

TABLE VIII.—QUANTITY of SEWAGE due to POPULATION.

Population.	Average Flow during 24 hours.			Maximum Flow, half in 6 hours.			Allowance for Rainfall for Population of 100 per acre, or 435 super. feet of area per inhabitant.		
	At 20 Galls. per Head.	At 30 Galls. per Head.	At 50 Galls. per Head.	At 20 Galls. per Head.	At 30 Galls. per Head.	At 50 Galls. per Head.	At ¼ Inch in 24 hours.	At ½ Inch in 24 Hours.	At 1 Inch in 24 hours.
	galls. per min.	galls. per min.	galls. per min.	galls. per min.	galls. per min.	galls. per min.	galls. per min.	galls. per min.	galls. per min.
500	7	10	17	14	21	35	19·6	39·3	·78·7
1,000	14	21	35	28	42	69	39	79	157
2,000	28	42	69	56	83	139	70	157	315
3,000	42	62	104	83	125	208	118	236	472
4,000	56	83	139	111	167	278	157	315	629
5,000	69	104	174	139	208	347	196	393	787
6,000	83	125	208	167	250	417	235	472	944
7,000	97	146	243	194	292	486	275	551	1,101
8,000	111	167	278	222	338	556	314	630	1,258
9,000	125	187	312	250	375	625	353	708	1,416
10,000	139	208	347	278	417	694	393	787	1,573
20,000	278	417	694	555	833	1,389	787	1,573	3,146
30,000	416	625	1,041	833	1,250	2,083	1,179	2,358	4,717
40,000	555	833	1,389	1,110	1,667	2,778	1,573	3,146	6,292
50,000	694	1,042	1,736	1,389	2,083	3,472	1,966	3,932	7,865

QUANTITY of SEWAGE due to POPULATION.

Population.	Average Flow during 24 hours.			Maximum Flow, half in 6 hours.			Allowance for Rainfall for Population of 100 per acre, or 435 super. feet of area per inhabitant.		
	At 20 Galls. per Head.	At 30 Galls. per Head.	At 50 Galls. per Head.	At 20 Galls. per Head.	At 30 Galls. per Head.	At 50 Galls. per Head.	At ¼ Inch in 24 Hours.	At ½ Inch in 24 Hours.	At 1 Inch in 24 Hours.
	galls. per min.	galls. per min.	galls. per min.	galls. per min.	galls. per min.	galls. per min.	galls. per min.	galls. per min.	galls. per min.
60,000	833	1,250	2,083	1,666	2,500	4,166	2,358	4,717	9,434
70,000	972	1,458	2,430	1,944	2,916	4,860	2,652	5,504	11,009
80,000	1,110	1,667	2,778	2,220	3,334	5,556	3,146	6,292	12,584
90,000	1,250	1,875	3,125	2,500	3,750	6,250	3,539	7,079	14,157
100,000	1,389	2,083	3,472	2,778	4,166	6,944	3,932	7,865	15,729

250 gallons per inhabited house, being about 44 gallons per head, is the quantity prescribed by Act of Parliament to be provided for in the Lower Thames Valley and Darenth Valley Main Sewerage Districts. This is understood to include some allowance for rainfall.

Rainfall should not be taken on the basis of population, as in the third column, unless *either* the whole area is to be provided for is continuously built upon, *or* the separate system is adopted and rain not admitted to the sewers except in close proximity to houses.

In the former case, if the population be greater than is assumed, the figures in the Table must obviously be *divided* by the ratio to 100 ; thus, for population of 200 per acre divide by 2, for 150 per acre take two-thirds, &c., and similarly for 50 per acre multiply by 2, &c.

On the other hand, if the system to be adopted is that of excluding the rain water, the average area pertaining to each inhabited house must first be ascertained and the number of persons per house ; and the figures in the third column may be adopted or will require modification, according as the result arrived at compares with the assumption of 435 super feet to each individual.

E

TABLE IX.—QUANTITY and DISCHARGE from AREAS due to RAINFALL.

Area.	Quantity equal to 1 Inch of Rain over Surface.	Equivalent Supply Daily throughout the Year.	Quantity running off at following Rates.							
			1 Inch in an hour.	½ Inch in an hour.	¼ Inch in an hour.	⅛ Inch in an hour.	1 Inch in 24 hours.	½ Inch in 24 hours.	¼ Inch in 24 hours.	⅛ Inch in 24 hours.
	gallons	gallons	galls. per min.	galls. per min.	galls. per min.	galls. per min.	galls. per min.	galls. per min.	galls. per min.	galls. per min.
100 sup. feet	52	0·14	0·87	0·43	0·22	0·11	0·036	0·018	0·009	0·005
200 „	104	0·28	1·74	0·87	0·43	0·22	0·072	0·036	0·018	0·009
300 „	156	0·43	2·60	1·30	0·65	0·32	0·108	0·054	0·027	0·013
400 „	208	0·57	3·47	1·74	0·87	0·43	0·144	0·072	0·036	0·018
500 „	260	0·71	4·34	2·17	1·08	0·54	0·181	0·090	0·045	0·022
1,000 „	520	1·4	8·7	4·3	2·2	1·1	0·36	0·18	0·09	0·05
2,000 „	1,040	2·8	17·4	8·7	4·3	2·2	0·72	0·36	0·18	0·09
3,000 „	1,560	4·3	26·0	13·0	6·5	3·2	1·08	0·54	0·27	0·13
4,000 „	2,080	5·7	34·7	17·4	8·7	4·3	1·44	0·72	0·36	0·18
5,000 „	2,600	7·1	43·4	21·7	10·8	5·4	1·81	0·90	0·45	0·22
10,000 „	5,200	14·2	86·8	43·4	21·7	10·8	3·62	1·81	0·90	0·45
1 acre	22,651	62	377	189	94	47	15·7	7·9	3·9	2·0
2 acres	45,302	124	755	377	189	94	31·5	15·7	7·9	3·9
3 „	67,954	186	1,132	566	284	142	47·2	23·6	11·8	5·9
4 „	90,605	248	1,510	755	378	189	63·0	31·5	15·7	7·9
5 „	113,256	310	1,887	944	472	236	78·7	39·3	19·6	9·8

QUANTITY and DISCHARGE from AREAS due to RAINFALL.

Area.	Quantity equal to 1 Inch of Rain over Surface.	Equivalent Supply Daily throughout the Year.	Quantity running off at following Rates.							
			1 Inch in an hour.	½ Inch in an hour.	¼ Inch in an hour.	⅛ Inch in an hour.	1 Inch in 24 hours.	½ Inch in 24 hours.	¼ Inch in 24 hours.	⅛ Inch in 24 hours.
	gallons	gallons	galls. per min.	galls. per min.	galls. per min.	galls. per min.	galls. per min.	galls. per min.	galls. per min.	galls. per min.
10 acres	226,512	620	3,775	1,888	944	472	157	79	39	20
20 "	453,025	1,241	7,550	3,775	1,888	944	315	157	79	39
30 "	679,537	1,862	11,326	5,663	2,831	1,415	472	236	118	59
40 "	906,049	2,482	15,101	7,550	3,776	1,888	629	315	157	79
50 "	1,132,561	3,103	18,876	9,438	4,719	2,360	787	393	196	98
100 "	2,265,122	6,206	37,752	18,876	9,438	4,719	1,573	787	393	196
200 "	4,530,245	12,412	75,504	37,752	18,876	9,438	3,146	1,573	787	393
300 "	6,795,367	18,618	113,256	56,628	28,314	14,152	4,717	2,358	1,179	589
400 "	9,060,490	24,823	151,008	75,504	37,752	18,876	6,292	3,145	1,573	787
500 "	11,325,612	31,029	188,760	94,380	47,190	23,595	7,865	3,932	1,966	983
1 square mile	14,496,770	39,717	241,613	120,806	60,403	30,201	10,067	5,033	2,516	1,258

It is estimated that on an average four-fifths of the Rain runs off slated roofs, one-half off streets and paved surfaces; and one-eighth part off the surface of cultivated land, within an hour of falling, whenever the fall is considerable.

E 2

TABLE X.—ANNUAL RAINFALL.

(1) Mean Annual Rainfall during thirty years (1850–1879) at forty-six Stations in British Isles.

County.	Place.	Height above Sea.	Mean Annual Rainfall.
		feet	inches
ENGLAND—			
Kent	Greenwich	155	25·2
Sussex	Uckfield	149	30·8
"	Chichester	284	33·5
Hertford	Hitchin	238	25·0
"	Berkhampstead	370	29·5
Bucks	High Wycombe	225	24·9
Northampton	Northampton	310	23·5
Bedford	Cardington	106	23·1
Norfolk	Norwich	137	25·8
Lincoln	Spalding	20	24·5
Shropshire	Shiffnal	353	26·5
Worcester	Tenbury	200	31·0
Devon	Exeter	140	31·1
ENGLAND (contd.)—			
Cornwall	Bodmin	315	47·7
Lancashire	Ormskirk	38	35·0
"	Stonyhurst	376	46·9
"	Bolton, The Fold	286	46·7
"	Bolton, Belmont	481	55·9
Yorkshire	Leeds	94	22·9
"	Redmires	1100	40·1
"	Standidge	1100	51·6
Northumberland	Whittle Dean	(?)	25·4
Cumberland	Keswick	270	58·8
"	Seathwaite	422	138·7
Westmoreland	Kendal	156	50·0

ANNUAL RAINFALL.

(1) Mean Annual Rainfall during thirty years (1850–1879) at forty-six Stations in British Isles.

County.	Place.	Height above Sea.	Mean Annual Rainfall.	County.	Place.	Height above Sea.	Mean Annual Rainfall.
		feet.	inches			feet.	inches
WALES—				SCOTLAND (contd.)—			
Carnarvon ..	Llandudno ..	99	32·80	Forfar	Dundee ..	50	36·0
Glamorgan ..	Cardiff	39	44·18	Ross	Cromarty ..	28	24·1
				Inverness ..	Inverness ..	104	25·1
SCOTLAND—				,,	Barrahead ..	640	31·9
Edinburgh ..	Inveresk	80	28·0	Sutherland ..	Cape Wrath ..	355	38·1
,,	Glencorse ..	787	38·3	Caithness ..	Noss Head ..	127	25·9
Lanark ..	Bothwell Castle	146	29·5				
Renfrew ..	Waulk Glen ..	280	47·4	IRELAND—			
Bute	Pladda	55	38·4	Cork	Cork ..	30	35·1
Argyle ..	Lismore	87	41·9	Kilkenny ..	Woodstock ..	400	40·8
,,	Ardnamurchan	82	43·5	King's County	Tullamore ..	235	27·8
,,	Rhinns of Islay	74	33·2	Armagh ..	Armagh ..	208	30·4
,,	Mull of Cantire	279	43·2				

ANNUAL RAINFALL.

(2) Mean Maximum and Minimum Annual Rainfall during fifty-two years (1830–82) at ten Stations in England.

Place.	Mean Annual Rainfall.	Maximum in one Year.		Minimum in one Year.		Minimum Average of Three Consecutive Years.	
	Inches		Inches		Inches		Inches
Greenwich ⋮ ⋮ ⋮	24·8	(1852)	34·0	(1864)	16·4	(1856–8)	20·1
Chichester ⋮ ⋮	33·6	,,	50·9	(1854)	21·8	(1854–6)	27·9
Hemel Hempstead ⋮ ⋮	26·8	,,	41·1	(1864)	17·0	(1862–4)	22·4
Oxford ⋮ ⋮ ⋮	23·4	,,	35·5	,,	14·8	,,	18·8
Tonbury ⋮ ⋮ ⋮	30·0	,,	45·4	(1854)	20·7	(1844–6)	25·4
Exeter ⋮ ⋮ ⋮	30·3	(1872)	46·0	,,	18·1	(1854–6)	21·4
Spalding ⋮ ⋮ ⋮	25·6	(1880)	37·1	(1874)	16·2	,,	20·8
Boston ⋮ ⋮ ⋮	22·7	,,	34·4	(1854)	13·8	(1853–5)	18·7
Bolton ⋮ ⋮ ⋮	47·4	(1831)	62·3	(1844)	34·6	(1855–7)	41·5
Kendal ⋮ ⋮ ⋮	51·5	(1872)	69·2	(1855)	34·5	(1854–6)	40·0

TABLE XI.—MONTHLY RAINFALL.

(1) Observations at Greenwich, 1841 to 1879.

Month.	Mean Fall during Thirty-nine Years. (Inches)	Maximum Fall in any One Year. (Inches)	Minimum Fall in any One Year. (Inches)	Minimum Falls in any Three, Four, and Six consecutive Months.
January	2·12	(1877) 4·35	(1861) 0·55	Minimum in three months:—
February	1·44	(1866) 4·03	(1857) 0·30	(April, May, June, 1870), 1·14 in.
March	1·47	(1851) 4·05	(1852) 0·17	(Feb., Mar., April, 1863), 1·65 in.
April	1·66	(1878) 4·31	(1855) 0·09	Minimum in four months:—
May	2·07	(1865) 4·37	(1844) 0·30	(Dec., 1873, to Mar., 1874), 2·70 in.
June	2·05	(1860) 5·80	(1849) 0·30	(Feb. to Mar., 1863), 2·90 in.
July	2·40	(1867) 5·81	(1864) 0·27	Minimum in six months:—
August	2·49	(1878) 5·38	(1849) 0·45	(Dec., 1873, to May, 1874), 4·47 in.
September	2·25	(1871) 4·12	(1865) 0·16	(Jan. to June, 1870), 5·22 in.
October	2·82	(1841) 5·95	(1879) 0·76	
November	2·23	(1852) 6·00	(1867) 0·42	
December	1·76	(1876) 5·76	(1873) 0·31	
Whole year	24·76	(1852) 34·01	(1864) 16·38	

(2) Observations at Glencorse, Edinburgh, 700 feet above sea, 1852 to 1882.

Month.	Mean Fall during Twenty-one Years.	Maximum Fall in any One Year.	Minimum Fall in any One Year.	Minimum Falls in any Three, Four, and Six consecutive Months.
	Inches	Inches	Inches	
January	4·20	(1863) 9·40	(1879) 1·70	Minimum in three months:—
February	3·03	(1868) 6·00	(1874) 1·20	(Feb., Mar., April, 1873), 3·30 in.
March	2·87	(1876) 6·10	(1863) 0·95	(Feb., Mar., April, 1865), 3·55 in.
April	2·58	(1880) 5·00	(1865–73) 0·40	
May	2·69	(1865) 6·00	(1871) 0·70	Minimum in four months :—
June	2·67	(1879) 6·20	(1865) 0·40	(March to June, 1873), 5·05 in.
July	3·57	(1879) 11·00	(1868) 0·55	(May to August, 1864), 6·55 in.
August	4·04	(1877) 9·60	(1864) 0·40	
September	3·55	(1872) 6·15	(1865) 0·70	Minimum of six months :—
October..	4·02	(1874) 9·90	(1866) 1·45	(Feb. to July, 1873), 10·30 in.
November	3·63	(1872–5) 5·75	(1867) 0·25	(Apr. to Sept., 1864), 10·50 in.
December	3·78	(1882) 8·45	(1870) 2·40	
Whole year	40 63	(1877) 54·30	(1870) 27·70	

TABLE XII.—DAILY and HOURLY MAXIMUM RAINFALL.

Period.	Greatest Ordinary Heavy Fall (as defined by Meteorological Society, all beyond this being recorded as " Extraordinary ").	Extraordinary Falls recorded during the Years 1879, 1880 and 1881.
hours		fall during the year.
24	2 inches, where the total fall during the year exceeds 33 iuches	5·42 at Sligachan, Skye.. .. 115·41 4·99 at Seathwaite .. .. 130·58 [Falls of 6·41 and 6·70 have been recorded at this Station in previous years.] 4·85 at Bridgend, Glamorgan 121·12 4·17 at Aberdare .. .. .. 98·83 3·91 at Neath.. .. .. .. 85·83
	6 per cent. of the fall during the year, where it does not exceed 33 inches	3·80 at Cambridge, being 12·3 p. c. of 30·96 3·75 at Huntingdon „ 11·8 „ 31·89 3·30 at Upwell „ 11·7 „ 28·14 3·57 at Stockton „ 11·4 „ 31·31 3·54 at Northallerton „ 10·8 „ 32·66 3·20 at Aboyne „ 10·6 „ 30·01
2	·83 inch, or at rate of ·42 per hour	3 inches = 1½ per hour. Rotherham, Sept. 15, 1880.
1¾	·82 inch, or at rate of ·49 per hour	
1½	·78 inch, or at rate of ·52 per hour	1·42 inches = ·94 per hour. Ross, Aug. 23, 1881.
1¼	·75 inch, or at rate of ·60 per hour	3·07 inches = 2·45 per hour! Athlone, June 25, 1880.
1	·70 inch	1·31 inches. Congleton, July 31, 1881.
min. 45	·60 inch, or at rate of ·80 per hour	
30	·50 inch, or at rate of 1 in. per hr.	2·90 inches = 5·80 per hour! Cowbridge, South Wales, July 22, 1880.
25	·44 inch, or at rate of 1·06 in. per hr.	1·18 inches = 2·18 per hour. Llandudno, May 26, 1881.
20	·40 inch, or at rate of 1·20 in. per hr.	1·48 inches = 4·44 per hour! Barnstaple, June 30, 1879.
15	·35 inch, or at rate of 1·40 in. per hr.	
10	·30 inch, or at rate of 1·80 in. per hr.	·41 inch = 2·46 per hour. Darlington, Jan. 11, 1881. ·51 inch = 3·40 per hour. Midmar (Aberdeen), Aug. 23, 1879.
5	·20 inch, or at rate of 2·40 in. per hr.	·31 inch in 5 minutes = 3·72 per hour. Sheffield, Aug. 17, 1879. ·27 inch in 3½ minutes = 4·63 per hour. London, June 24, 1879.

TABLE XIII.—WATER SUPPLY by GRAVITATION—
NOTE.—Dimensions of Service Reservoirs and Distributing

Population.	Supply Required at 20 Gallons per Head.		Area of Gathering Ground for 12 Inches Available Rainfall.	Storage Reservoir to Hold Supply for 150 Days.
	Daily.	Equivalent per Minute.		
	gallons	gallons	acres	
500	10,000	7	13½	175 ft. diam. by 10 ft. deep
1,000	20,000	14	27	226 „ 12 „
2,000	40,000	28	53⅓	320 „ 12 „
3,000	60,000	42	80½	{ 391 „ 12 „ } { 2¾ acres by 12 „ }
5,000	100,000	70	134	3¾ „ 15 „
6,000	120,000	84	161	4½ „ 15 „
8,000	160,000	112	215	6 „ 15 „
10,000	200,000	139	268	{ 7½ „ 15 „ } { 5½ „ 20 „ }
20,000	400,000	278	536	{ 15 „ 15 „ } { 11 „ 20 „ }
30,000	600,000	417	805	16½ „ 20 „
50,000	1,000,000	694	1340	27½ „ 20 „
60,000	1,200,000	833	1610	33 „ 20 „
80,000	1,600,000	1,111	2145	44 „ 20 „
			sq. miles	
100,000	2,000,000	1,389	4·2	{ 55 „ 20 „ } { 44 „ 25 „ }
500,000	10,000,000	6,944	21	{ 220 „ 25 „ } { 183 „ 30 „ }
1,000,000	20,000,000	13,889	42	{ 440 „ 25 „ } { 367 „ 30 „ }

WORKS for GIVEN POPULATION.

Mains same as for Pumping Works. (See next page.)

Filter Beds to Pass 600 Gallons per Super. Yard in 24 Hours, allowing for one not in use.	Main Conduit to Pass Supply in 24 Hours, flowing continuously.
No. 2, each 15 ft. by 10 ft.	1½ inch, loss of head 1 in 120 2 " " 1 " 400
" " 20 " 15 "	2 " " 1 " 120 3 " " 1 " 1000
No. 3, " 30 " 10 "	3 " " 1 " 240 4 " " 1 " 1000
" " 30 " 15 "	4 " " 1 " 450 5 " " 1 " 1200
" " 50 " 15 "	4 " " 1 " 160 6 " " 1 " 1200
" " 50 " 18 "	5 " " 1 " 350 6 " " 1 " 900
" " 60 " 20 "	6 " " 1 " 500 7 " " 1 " 1000
No. 4, " 50 " 20 " or 32 ft. sq.	6 " " 1 " 300 8 " " 1 " 1250
No. 4, each 45 ft. square ..	9 " " 1 " 600 10 " " 1 " 1000
" " 55 " ..	10 " " 1 " 450 12 " " 1 " 1000
" " 70 " ..	12 " " 1 " 400 15 " " 1 " 1200
" " 76 " ..	12 " " 1 " 275 15 " " 1 " 850
" " 90 " ..	15 " " 1 " 480 18 " " 1 " 1200
No. 6 " 77½ " ..	18 " " 1 " 750 21 " " 1 " 1700
" " 173 " ..	2½ feet, " 1 " 400 3 " " 1 " 1000
" " 245 " ..	3 " " 1 " 250 4 " " 1 " 1000

TABLE XIV.—WATER SUPPLY by PUMPING—

Population.	Supply Required at 20 Gallons per Head.		Hours during which it is proposed to Pump.	Net Horse-power to raise to 100 Feet Elevation.
	Daily.	Equivalent per Minute.		
500	gallons 10,000	gallons 7	4	1½
1,000	20,000	14	6	1¾
2,000	40,000	28	10	2
3,000	60,000	42	10	3
5,000	100,000	70	10	5
6,000	120,000	84	10	6
8,000	160,000	112	10	8
10,000	200,000	139	10	10⅛
20,000	400,000	278	18	11¼
30,000	600,000	417	24	12⅔
50,000	1,000,000	694	24	21
60,000	1,200,000	833	24	25¼
80,000	1,600,000	1,111	24	33½
100,000	2,000,000	1,389	24	42
500,000	10,000,000	6,944	24	210
1,000,000	20,000,000	13,889	24	421

WORKS for GIVEN POPULATION.

Dimensions of Single Pump, working 10 Strokes per Minute.			Dimensions of Pumping Main.		Service Reservoir to hold Three Days' Supply.			Main Delivery Pipe to Pass at Rate of One-half in Four Hours.	
Diam	Stroke.		Diam.	Loss of Head.				Diam.	Loss of Head.
in.	ft.	in.	in.					in.	
8	2	0	3	1 in 110	22 ft. sq. by 10 ft. deep			3	1 in 400
9	2	0	4	1 „ 450	31	„	10 „	4	1 „ 450
10	2	0	5	1 „ 500	40	„	12 „	5	1 „ 350
12	2	1	5	1 „ 240	49	„	12 „	6	1 „ 380
14	2	6	6	1 „ 220	56½	„	15 „	8	1 „ 580
15	2	8	7	1 „ 330	62	„	15 „	8	1 „ 400
16	3	0	8	1 „ 350	71½	„	15 „	9	1 „ 400
18	3	1	9	1 „ 400	80	„	15 „	10	1 „ 450
18	3	4½	9	1 „ 335	98	„	20 „	15	1 „ 850
18	3	9	10	1 „ 450	120	„	20 „	15	1 „ 440
21	5	0	12	1 „ 400	155	„	20 „	18	1 „ 310
24	4	3	15	1 „ 850	170	„	20 „	21	1 „ 500
24	5	8	15	1 „ 475	196	„	20 „	24	1 „ 570
24	7	0	18	1 „ 770	220	„	20 „	27	1 „ 650
			ft. in.					ft. in.	
3·9	10	0	2 6	1 „ 385	438	„	25 „	4 0	1 „ 500
5·0	11	4	3 0	1 „ 245	620	„	25 „	6 0	1 „ 880

TABLE XV.—ANALYSIS OF WATER.

Results in parts per 100,000. To convert the figures in columns 1 to 6 into grains per gallon (which is a usual measure with these substances), multiply by seven-tenths. Grains per gallon of Hardness (columns 3, 4, and 5) are generally described as "degrees of hardness."

Source or Description of Water.	(1) Total Solid Matter in Solution.	(2) Temporary Hardness.	(3) Permanent Hardness.	(4) Total Hardness.	(5) Chlorine.	(6) Organic Carbon.	(7) Organic Nitrogen.	(8) Ammonia.	(9) Nitrogen in Nitrates.	(10) Free Ammonia by Distillation.	(11) Albuminoid Ammonia by Distillation.
Rain Water (average)	2·9	··	··	0·3	0·2	·070	·015	·029	·003	··	··
Glasgow (Loch Katrine)	3·1	··	··	1·0	0·7	·132	·014	·000	·003	·000	·008
Edinburgh (gathering grounds)	8·9	0·0	4·7	4·7	0·9	·638	·034	·005	·000	·000	·007
Whitehaven (Ennerdale Lake)	2·2	0·0	1·45	1·4	1·0	·042	·017	·000	·000	··	··
Sunderland (deep well in Dolomite)	44·2	0·8	13·9	14·7	4·2	·035	·030	·000	·416	·003	·002
Liverpool (Green Lane Well, New Red Sandstone)	26·4	4·0	9·5	13·5	2·7	·020	·020	·000	·416	··	··
Ditto (Rivington Pike gathering grounds)	8·5	0·1	3·6	3·7	1·5	·243	·031	·004	·000	·031	·006
Manchester (gathering grounds)	6·2	0·1	3·6	3·7	1·1	·18	·009	·006	·025	··	··
St. Helens (deep well in New Red Sandstone)	21·7	5·9	6·8	12·7	1·9	·00	·000	·000	·436	··	··
Oldham (gathering grounds)	12·8	0·0	0·0	6·9	1·3	·166	·014	·011	·011	·003	··
Ashton-under-Lyne (gathering grounds)	24·1	3·2	11·0	14·2	1·9	·200	·031	·010	·028	··	·012
Leicester (gathering grounds)	26·3	15·8	9·0	24·8	1·5	·485	·075	·001	·005	··	··

Birkenhead (deep well in New Red Sandstone)	18·8	0·15	9·7	9·8	3·4	·041	·038	·000	·366	·000	·002
Norwich (River Wensum)	30·9	21·3	5·3	26·6	3·1	·432	·080	·014	·036		
Tewkesbury (River Severn)	19·3	0·0	10·0	10·0	3·5	·405	·043	·000	·041		
Chester (River Dee)	16·8	5·0	3·7	10·7	2·0	·219	·043	·000	·000	·000	·007
Bedford (River Ouse)	47·9	13·5	15·0	28·5	2·7	·620	·088	·004			
Northampton (deep wells in Lias Limestone)	57·8	8·6	1·7	10·3	5·15	·168	·024	·003	·000		
Croydon (deep wells in Chalk)	32·0	12·9	9·1	22·0		·400	·070	·001	·551	·001	·001
Tring (deep wells in Chalk)	28·6	22·9	3·3	26·2	1·39	·036	·010	·001	·094		
Ditto, after softening by Clark's process	8·2	0·0	3·2	3·2	1·19	·041	·008	·001			
Eastbourne (deep well in Hastings Sand)	43·1	13·8	7·1	20·9	10·0	·058	·010	·004	·130		
London Companies, July to Oct. 1883—											
West Middlesex (Thames)	25·8			19·2	1·50	·138	·021	·000	·166	·001	·005
Southwark and Vauxhall (Thames)	29·4			19·9	1·55	·158	·023	·000	·178	·002	·005
New River (River Lea and Wells)	26·7			19·9	1·55	·073	·018	·000	·212	·002	·003
East London (River Lea)	27·2			19·6	1·70	·115	·026	·000	·182	·004	·005
Kent (deep wells in Chalk)	40·3			28·7	2·60	·042	·017	·000	·475	·003	·003
Artesian Well, Trafalgar Square)	83·4	2·9	2·9	5·9	16·5	·050	·012	·070	·000		
Thames at London Bridge	34			27	1·8	·30	·03	·12	·17	·102	·059
Irwell at Salford	55			23	9·6	1·17	·33	·74	·71		
Croydon Sewage (raw)	46*			32	4·2	2·51	1·58	3·00	·00	55·0	3·0
Ditto, after passing Sewage Farm	38			27	2·7	0·64	0·13	0·13	·375	0·63	0·08
Sea Water	3898	49	748	797	1975	0·28	0·16	·006	·033		

* These figures are exclusive of suspended matter.

TABLE XVI.—QUANTITY of BRICKWORK in CIRCULAR SEWERS,
CULVERTS, or WELLS.

NOTE.—The quantity of earth displaced will be the sum of the
contents and brickwork added together.

Internal Diameter.	Contents of One Lineal Yard.	Brickwork per Lineal Yard.		Internal Diameter.	Contents of One Lineal Yard.	Brickwork per Lineal Yard.	
		4½ Inches Thick.	9 Inches Thick.			9 Inches Thick.	14 Inches Thick.
ft. in.	cub. ft.	cub. ft.	cub. ft.	ft. in.	cub. ft.	cub. ft.	cub. ft.
1 6	5·3	6·6	15·9	6 0	84·8	47·7	75·6
1 9	7·2	7·5	17·7	6 6	99·5	51·2	80·8
2 0	9·4	8·4	19·4	7 0	115·5	54·8	86·1
2 3	11·9	9·3	21·2	7 6	132·5	58·3	91·3
2 6	14·7	10·1	23·0	8 0	150·8	61·8	96·8
2 9	17·8	11·0	24·7	8 6	170·2	65·4	102·1
3 0	21·2	11·9	26·5	9 0	190·9	68·9	107·4
3 3	24·9	12·7	28·3	9 6	212·6	72·4	112·7
3 6	28·9	13·7	30·0	10 0	235·6	76·0	118·0
3 9	33·1	14·6	31·8	11 0	285·1	83·1	128·5
4 0	37·6	15·5	33·6	12 0	339·3	90·0	139·1
4 6	47·7	17·2	37·1	13 0	398·2	97·2	149·8
5 0	58·9	19·0	40·6	14 0	461·8	104·2	160·35
5 6	71·3	20·7	44·2	15 0	530·1	111·3	171·0

TABLE XVII.—QUANTITY of BRICKWORK in EGG-SHAPED SEWERS.

Internal Dimensions.	Contents of One Lineal Yard.	Brickwork per Lineal Yard.		Internal Dimensions.	Contents of One Lineal Yard.	Brickwork per Lineal Yard.	
		4½ In. Thick.	9 In. Thick.			4½ In. Thick.	9 In. Thick.
ft. in. ft. in.	cub. ft.	cub. ft.	cub. ft.	ft. in. ft. in.	cub. ft.	cub. ft.	cub. ft.
2 0×1 4	6·0	7·4	16·5	3 6×2 4	18·5	11·6	25·5
2 3×1 6	8·2	8·1	18·8	3 9×2 6	21·2	12·4	26·9
2 6×1 8	9·4	8·8	20·1	4 0×2 8	24·2	13·0	28·3
2 9×1 10	11·4	9·5	21·4	4 6×3 0	32·9	14·4	31·1
3 0×2 0	13·6	10·2	22·7	5 0×3 4	37·7	15·8	34·0
3 3×2 2	15·9	10·9	24·0	6 0×4 0	54·2	18·8	39·4

In egg-shaped sewers about one-seventh part of the brickwork forms
the invert, three-sevenths the top, and three-sevenths the sides. The
two former should generally be built with radiating bricks of the
radius required in each case.

TABLE XVIII.—WEIGHT of CAST-IRON PIPES.

NOTE.—The weight includes proportion due to sockets, pipes of 2 and 2½ inches diameter being in 6-feet lengths, pipes 3 to 12 inches inclusive in 9-feet lengths, and those of larger size in 12-feet lengths, exclusive of socket.

Internal Diameter of Pipe.	For Pressure not exceeding 150 Feet.		For Pressure not exceeding 300 Feet.		For Pressure not exceeding 500 Feet.	
	Thickness of Metal.	Weight per Yard.	Thickness of Metal.	Weight per Yard.	Thickness of Metal.	Weight per Yard.
inches	inch	cwt. qrs. lbs.	inch	cwt. qrs. lbs.	inch	cwt. qrs. lbs.
2	$\frac{9}{32}$	0 2 24	$\frac{4}{16}$	0 0 26	$\frac{11}{32}$	0 1 0
2½	$\frac{5}{16}$	0 1 0	$\frac{11}{32}$	0 1 2	$\frac{3}{8}$	0 1 6
3	$\frac{5}{16}$	0 1 5	$\frac{11}{32}$	0 1 9	$\frac{3}{8}$	0 1 14
4	$\frac{11}{32}$	0 1 22	$\frac{3}{8}$	0 1 26	$\frac{7}{16}$	0 2 5
5	$\frac{3}{8}$	0 2 14	$\frac{7}{16}$	0 2 21	$\frac{1}{2}$	0 3 4
6	$\frac{3}{8}$	0 2 21	$\frac{7}{16}$	0 3 5	$\frac{1}{2}$	0 3 21
7	$\frac{7}{16}$	0 3 24	$\frac{1}{2}$	1 0 12	$\frac{9}{16}$	1 1 0
8	$\frac{7}{16}$	1 0 12	$\frac{1}{2}$	1 1 0	$\frac{9}{16}$	1 1 21
9	$\frac{1}{2}$	1 1 12	$\frac{9}{16}$	1 2 2	$\frac{5}{8}$	1 2 21
10	$\frac{1}{2}$	1 2 0	$\frac{9}{16}$	1 2 21	$\frac{5}{8}$	1 3 14
12	$\frac{9}{16}$	2 0 0	$\frac{5}{8}$	2 0 25	$\frac{11}{16}$	2 1 21
14	$\frac{5}{8}$	2 2 18	$\frac{11}{16}$	2 3 21	$\frac{3}{4}$	3 0 21
15	$\frac{5}{8}$	2 3 7	$\frac{11}{16}$	.3 0 10	$\frac{13}{16}$	3 2 14
16	$\frac{11}{16}$	3 0 0	$\frac{3}{4}$	3 2 9	$\frac{7}{8}$	4 0 21
18	$\frac{11}{16}$	3 3 0	$\frac{3}{4}$	4 0 0	$\frac{15}{16}$	4 3 21
21	$\frac{13}{16}$	4 1 0	$\frac{13}{16}$	5 0 0	1	6 1 14
24	$\frac{3}{4}$	5 1 0	$\frac{7}{8}$	6 1 0	$1\frac{1}{8}$	8 0 0
27	$\frac{3}{4}$	6 0 0	$\frac{15}{16}$	7 2 0	$1\frac{3}{16}$	9 1 0
30	$\frac{7}{8}$	7 3 14	1	8 3 21	$1\frac{1}{4}$	11 1 0
36	1	10 2 21	$1\frac{1}{8}$	11 2 14	$1\frac{1}{2}$	15 3 14

TABLE XIX.—WEIGHT of LEAD PIPES.

NOTE.—Columns 1, 2, and 3 are the pipes usually known as "common," "middling," and "strong" respectively; the figures in parenthesis show the weights per length of the coil according to which they are generally specified.

The "common" are available only for pipes with open ends, the "middling" for very slight pressures, and the "strong" for pressure of about 50 feet.

Column 4 are the weights prescribed by the Metropolis Water Act, 1871, and by the regulations of very many towns, and are available for pressures up to 200 feet or thereabouts.

Column 5 are those prescribed at Norwich and some other towns where the pressure is unusually great.

Internal Diameter of Pipe.	Weight per Yard in Lbs.				
	No. 1.	No. 2.	No. 3.	No. 4.	No. 5.
3/8 inch	.. ..	.. ..	.. ..	5	5½
½ "	3⅓ (16 lbs. to 15 ft.)	4⅖ (22 lbs. to 15 ft.)	5⅕ (26 lbs. to 15 ft.)	6	7
⅝ "	.. ..	.. ..	.. ..	7½	9
¾ "	4⅘ (24 lbs. to 15 ft.)	5⅗ (28 lbs. to 15 ft.)	7⅕ (36 lbs. to 15 ft.)	9	11
1 "	6 (30 lbs. to 15 ft.)	8 (40 lbs. to 15 ft.)	9⅗ (46 lbs. to 15 ft.)	12	16
1¼ "	9 (36 lbs. to 12 ft.)	11 (44 lbs. to 12 ft.)	13 (53 lbs. to 12 ft.)	16	22½
1½ "	12 (48 lbs. to 12 ft.)	14 (56 lbs. to 12 ft.)	17½ (70 lbs. to 12 ft.)	24	33

LONDON: PRINTED BY WILLIAM CLOWES AND SONS, LIMITED,
STAMFORD STREET AND CHARING CROSS.

www.ingramcontent.com/pod-product-compliance
Lightning Source LLC
Chambersburg PA
CBHW030716110426
42739CB00030B/651